MAPUCHE
SPIRITUALITY

MAPUCHE SPIRITUALITY

Prabhuji

MAPUCHE SPIRITUALITY
by Prabhuji

Copyright © 2026
First edition

Printed in Round Top, New York, United States

All rights reserved. None of the information contained in this book may be reproduced, republished, or re-disseminated in any manner or form without the prior written consent of the publisher.

Published by Prabhuji Mission
Website: prabhuji.net

Avadhutashram
PO Box 900
Cairo, NY, 12413
USA

Painting on the cover by Prabhuji:
"Mapuche Spirituality"
Mixed media on wood board, New York, USA, 2024
Size: 30"x40"

Library of Congress Control Number: 2025925862
ISBN-13: 978-1-945894-92-3

Contents

Preface 1

Chapter 1: Introduction to the Mapuche cosmovision 7
Chapter 2: Sacred nature in Mapuche culture 21
Chapter 3: The role of the *machi* in Mapuche shamanism.......... 35
Chapter 4: Fundamental rites of Mapuche spirituality 47
Chapter 5: Shamanic practices and spiritual healing................. 57
Chapter 6: The connection with the afterlife in
  Mapuche spirituality... 69
Chapter 7: Contemporary challenges of Mapuche spirituality..... 81
Chapter 8: Final reflections on Mapuche spirituality
  and shamanism.. 95

Appendices

About Prabhuji... 109
The term *prabhuji* by Swami Ramananda 127
The term *avadhūta* 131
About the Prabhuji Mission.. 145
About the Avadhutashram 149
The Retroprogressive Path 151
Prabhuji today... 153
Titles by Prabhuji... 157

ॐ अज्ञानतिमिरान्धस्य ज्ञानाञ्जनशलाकया ।
चक्षुरुन्मीलितं येन तस्मै श्रीगुरवे नमः ॥

oṁ ajñāna-timirāndhasya
jñānāñjana-śalākayā
cakṣur unmīlitaṁ yena
tasmai śrī-gurave namaḥ

Salutations unto that holy Guru who, applying the ointment [medicine] of [spiritual] knowledge, removes the darkness of ignorance of the blinded [unenlightened] and opens their eyes.

This book is dedicated, with deep gratitude and eternal respect, to the holy lotus feet of my beloved masters His Divine Grace Bhakti-kavi Atulānanda Ācārya Mahārāja (Gurudeva) and His Divine Grace Avadhūta Śrī Brahmānanda Bābājī Mahārāja (Guru Mahārāja).

Preface

The story of my life is an odyssey from what I believed myself to be to what I truly am... an inner and outer pilgrimage. A journey from the personal to the universal, from the partial to the whole, from the illusory to the real, from the apparent to the true. A wandering flight from the human to the divine.

Everything that awakens at dawn rests at dusk; every lit flame eventually extinguishes. Only what begins, ends; only what starts, finishes. But what dwells in the present is neither born nor dies, for that which lacks a beginning never perishes.

As a simple autobiographer and narrator of significant experiences, I share my intimate story with others. My story is not public but profoundly private and intimate. It does not belong to the turmoil of social life, but is a sigh kept in the most hidden depths of the soul.

I am a disciple of seers, enlightened beings, shadows of the universe who are nobody and walk in death. I am just a whim or perhaps a joke from the heavens and the only mistake of my beloved spiritual masters. I was initiated in my spiritual childhood by the moonlight, which showed me its light and shared its being with me. My muse was a seagull that loved to fly more than anything else in life.

In love with the impossible, I traversed the universe, obsessed with the brilliance of a star. I traveled countless paths, following the traces and vestiges of those with the vision to decipher the hidden. Like the ocean that longs for water, I sought my home within my own house.

I do not claim to be a guide, coach, teacher, instructor, educator, psychologist, enlightener, pedagogue, evangelist, rabbi, *posek halacha*, healer, therapist, satsangist, psychic, leader, medium, savior, guru, or authority of any kind, whether spiritual or material. I allow myself the audacity and daring to represent nothing and no one but myself. I am only a traveler whom you can ask for directions. With pleasure, I point you to a place where everything calms upon arrival... beyond the sun and the stars, your desires and longings, time and space, concepts and conclusions, and beyond all that you believe you are or imagine you will be.

I paint sighs, hopes, silences, aspirations, and melancholies, inner landscapes, and sunsets of the soul. I am a painter of the indescribable, inexpressible, and indefinable, and unconfessable of our depths... or maybe I just write colors and paint words. Aware of the abyss that separates revelation and works, I live in a frustrated attempt to faithfully express the mystery of the spirit.

Since childhood, little windows of paper captivated my attention; through them, I visited places, met people, and made friends. Those tiny mandalas were my true elementary school, high school, and college. Like skilled teachers, these *yantras* have guided me through contemplation, attention, concentration, observation, and meditation.

Like a physician studies the human body, or a lawyer studies laws, I have dedicated my entire life to the study of myself. I can say with certainty that I know what resides and lives in this heart.

My purpose is not to persuade others. It is not my intention to convince anyone of anything. I do not offer theology or philosophy, nor do I preach or teach, I simply think out loud. The echo of these words may lead you to the infinite space of peace, silence, love, existence, consciousness, and absolute bliss.

Do not search for me. Search for yourself. You do not need me or anyone else, because the only thing that really matters is you. What you yearn for lies within you, as what you are, here and now.

I am not a merchant of rehashed information, nor do I intend to do business with my spirituality. I do not teach beliefs or philosophies. I only speak about what I see and just share what I know.

Avoid fame, for true glory is not based on public opinion but on what you really are. What matters is not what others think of you, but your own appreciation of who you are.

Choose bliss over success, life over reputation, and wisdom over information. If you succeed, you will know not only admiration but also true envy. Jealousy is mediocrity's tribute to talent and an open acceptance of one's own inferiority.

I advise you to fly freely and never be afraid of making mistakes. Learn the art of transforming your mistakes into lessons. Never blame others for your faults: remember that taking complete responsibility for your life is a sign of maturity. Flying teaches you that what matters is not touching the sky but having the courage to spread your wings. The higher you rise, the more graciously small and insignificant the world will seem. As you walk, sooner or later you will understand that every search begins and ends in you.

Your unconditional well-wisher,

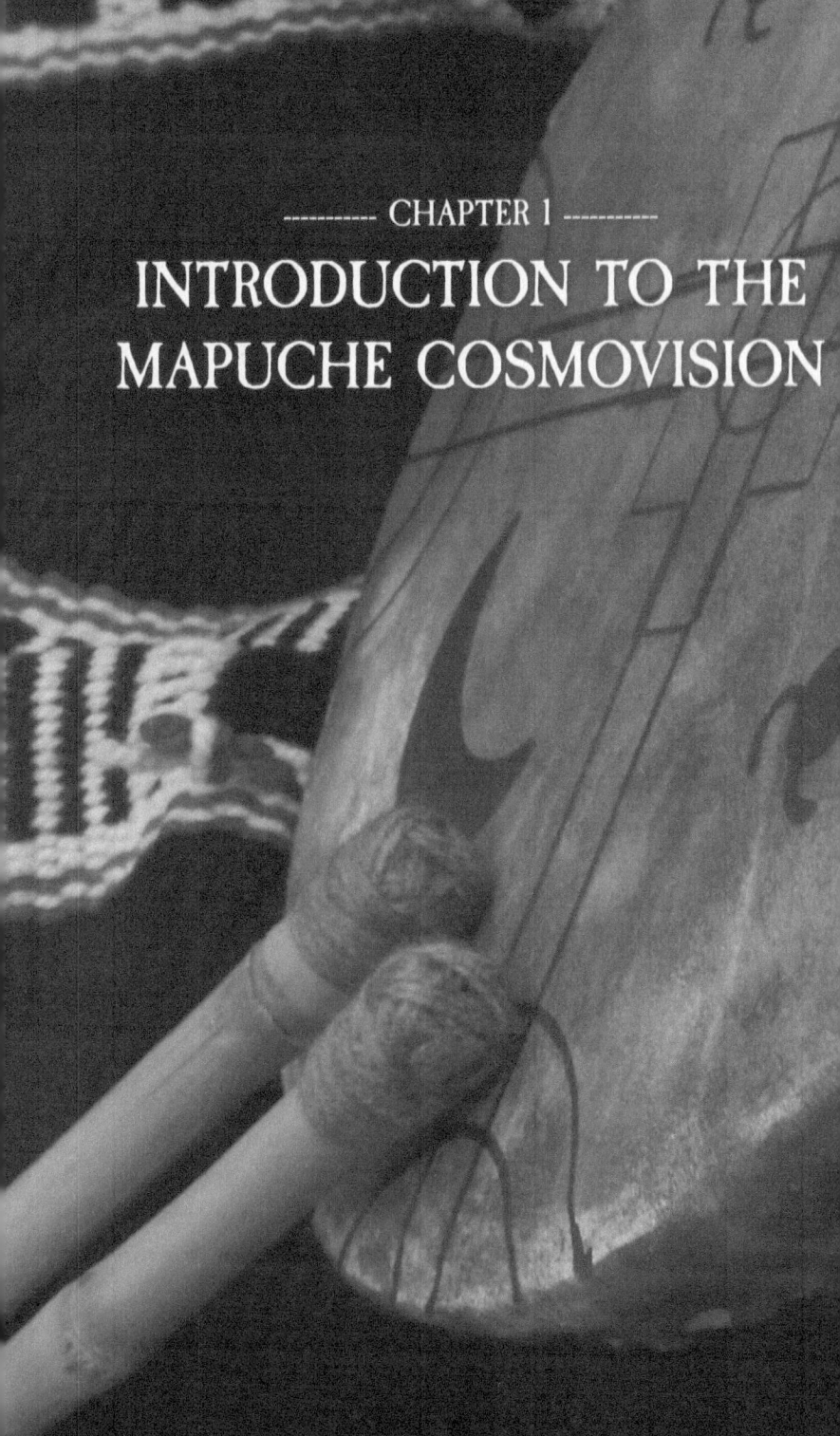

CHAPTER 1
INTRODUCTION TO THE MAPUCHE COSMOVISION

This book is born from my admiration and respect for the traditions, language, and ways of life of the Mapuche people. Since my youth in Chile, I have been captivated by the richness of their cultural heritage and the depth of their spirituality. In 1974, at the age of sixteen, I traveled to the Araucanía region to understand the life and values that have sustained this ancestral community. What began as a personal exploration soon became a transformative experience, an immersion that profoundly affected my worldview and left an indelible mark on my life. I am grateful to the extraordinary people of Loncoche, Curacautín, and Lumaco, who generously shared their knowledge and guided me on an invaluable journey through Mapuche wisdom.

Identity and history

The Mapuche worldview is based on a symbolic relationship with the natural environment, which shapes their values, cultural customs, and human relationships. It is a source of integral wisdom that regulates both the everyday aspects of life and their vital ceremonies. To understand this nation, we must delve into its history. They have had to defend their beliefs and territories against colonization and cultural assimilation. They have faced external threats without losing their sense of belonging and their respect for the environment. This perspective, anchored in centuries of tradition and resistance, continues to shape Mapuche identity today.

Chapter 1: Introduction to the Mapuche cosmovision

The Mapuche call themselves "people of the land" (from *mapu*, or "land," and *che*, or "person"), a term that reflects their perception of themselves as caretakers of the land. This sense of belonging is linked to their ancestral origin in southern South America, located in the area that is currently central and southern Chile and southwestern Argentina. Their relationship with the land goes beyond material dependence into the realm of the sacred.

Historical and archaeological records show that the Mapuche had a developed social structure in the sixteenth century when the Spanish conquistadors arrived in their territory. Like most indigenous cultures, they never formed a centralized polity. Instead, they were organized into autonomous units called *lof*. Each *lof* was led by a *lonko*, a leader in charge of managing both the political and cultural cohesion of the community. This decentralized organization allowed them to remain remarkably flexible, a key factor in resisting the colonial threat. The values of each *lof* promoted harmonious coexistence between humans and the natural environment, a principle that has endured for centuries as the foundation of their collective identity.

The first conflicts with the Spanish began in 1541, led by Pedro de Valdivia. This marked the beginning of a long period of resistance. Despite Spanish military incursions and cultural assimilation strategies, the Mapuche managed to resist and develop effective tactics for protecting their way of life. The protracted Arauco

War, which spanned more than three centuries, is a testament to this. In 1641, a peace treaty was signed that recognized Mapuche autonomy south of the Biobío River, an exceptional achievement in the history of indigenous resistance to colonialism.

During the nineteenth century, as Chile and Argentina consolidated as young nations, they faced a new wave of threats. The military campaigns known as the Pacification of Araucanía in Chile and the Conquest of the Desert in Argentina aimed to colonize the ancestral territory of numerous indigenous tribes. The loss of land eroded the network of meanings and knowledge that linked soils, rivers, animals, and other essential elements.

Faced with this invasion, the Mapuche people developed strategies that have been key to their enduring resistance. Over generations, they have managed to keep their worldview alive, despite being radically different from the imposed European paradigm. Their care for the environment and preservation of community are acts of resistance against foreign ideas. Human existence is closely linked to nature and to higher forces that influence physical reality and coexist with it. There are no rigid divisions between different dimensions of reality; on the contrary, interactions between humans and non-humans are constant and reciprocal. This vision fosters a common identity in which the community is the nucleus of knowledge transmission and intergenerational learning.

Chapter 1: Introduction to the Mapuche cosmovision

Mapuche identity is not limited to an ethnic classification but is manifested as a symbolic relationship with the environment as well as the tradition and wisdom that have endured centuries of colonization. This represents a model of resistance that is still relevant today. For the Mapuche, and for those seeking alternatives to the modern paradigm of resource exploitation, their attitude offers a model of respect and coexistence that can address our current ecological and cultural crises.

Cosmovision and conception of the universe

The Mapuche cosmovision articulates all beings and phenomena in an dynamic, interrelated, and interdependent whole. It does not reduce existence to isolated categories or utilitarian resources; rather, it considers each element—human, animal, plant, and mineral—to be an entity with intrinsic meaning within the greater cosmic system. The Mapuche perceive the universe as a vast space of symbolic and energetic relationships, where everything has its place and purpose, an ethical and mystical symmetry that regulates the balance of the world.

To understand this, we must explore *mapu*, a notion of space that transcends physical location. The land is the place where people inhabit and extract resources, but it is also a sentient being that sustains and nourishes all life. This vision is accompanied by an ethical and moral commitment: the Mapuche feel they must respect and preserve the land, because it is both a means and an end in itself. Each natural element is a node connected to the invisible forces that structure reality. The *mapu* is thus manifested as a sacred space, whose conservation and respect are essential to maintain the harmony of the whole.

The Mapuche idea of time is unlike Western linear time. Instead, it is a cycle, a recurrence of events and seasons that mark the constant renewal of life. In each cycle, the symbolic pact with the environment is renewed and the interdependence of all entities is recognized. This temporal cycle guides time and reaffirms their relationship with the universe and its natural rhythms, which generate a constant flow of renewal and continuity.

The Mapuche worldview structures the universe into four distinct levels that interact constantly, giving a sense of wholeness and correspondence between the visible and invisible planes of existence. At the highest level is *Wenu Mapu*, or "land above," where ancestors and deities who guide and protect the community dwell. Certain ancestors who attained a transcendent degree of purity and wisdom also live there. Among these beings is Ngenechén, a central divine figure who is not a distant creator, but a close presence who protects universal balance. His influence permeates all aspects of life, including people's health, the success of harvests, and natural phenomena. He is an object of veneration, and his presence is manifested in the environment through a symbolic language that the Mapuche interpret and respect in their daily actions.

Below the upper level is *Anka Wenu*, an intermediate zone occupied by *ngen* and *pillans*. *Ngen* are guardians of nature and control specific natural features such as mountains, rivers, and forests. They actively protect territories and must be respected. They respond to human actions, either by protecting those who honor the environment or punishing those who desecrate it. *Pillans* are like watchdogs that restore balance when necessary and respond with storms, eruptions, or droughts if the natural order is disrespected.

Below that, human life takes place on *mapu*, where there is direct interaction between the physical and natural worlds. This space is more than a stage for everyday life: it is the realm where humanity and nature are intertwined in a reciprocal relationship. The Mapuche understand that any action in the *mapu*, from agriculture to construction, must be done with due reverence toward the earth. Mapuche medicine is based on this principle: illnesses are both physical ailments and signs of spiritual imbalance. The *machi* are the healers and spiritual guides of the community. She has extensive knowledge of the properties of plants and the ritual techniques necessary to restore this harmony, seeking both physical and spiritual well-being.

Finally, *Minche Mapu* is deep underground, which is home to forces that are sometimes perceived as potentially conflicting, but are not considered inherently harmful. This is the home of the *wekufe*, who can cause imbalances if not treated carefully. Dealing with them requires respect, since these beings represent the chaotic aspects of reality, necessary to maintain the wholeness of the cosmos. *Machis* are important here, since their knowingness allows them to mediate between the community and these subterranean forces. Through purification and protection rituals, they ensure that the *wekufe* do not disturb the peace and order on the *mapu*. Disorder is not interpreted as being negative; rather, it is conceived as a complementary force that forms part of the universe's balance. The duality between order and chaos configures this worldview rich in nuances and symbolic relationships. Respect for each level and entity ensures cosmic balance, and this is part of how the Mapuche live according to the natural and spiritual rhythms that define their existence.

Ultimately, the Mapuche worldview is an invitation to understand the world as a web in which human beings are only one part of a larger mosaic. We must live with respect for each entity that inhabits the cosmos. From the ancestors in the *Wenu Mapu* to the *wekufe* in the *Minche Mapu*, each force and each level of existence are essential elements in the preservation of life and the maintenance of balance.

Ethical values and spirituality

Values and ethical principles come from a holistic and relational vision of existence, in which each element, whether human, natural, or symbolic, is intertwined

Chapter 1: Introduction to the Mapuche cosmovision

with the others. This interdependent network regulates both individual and collective behaviors and demands respect for the visible and invisible, tangible and intangible elements. Balance and reciprocity are not merely desirable values; they are essential conditions for the subsistence, harmony and continuity of the community over time. Thus, each act, no matter how small, is part of a system that goes beyond the individual and has repercussions for the community and nature as a whole. This means people have an ethical duty that guides their relationship with the environment and future generations.

Within this network of interdependencies and duties, the concept of *ngen mapu* stands out as a fundamental ethical principle that regulates the interaction with the land, the *mapu*. This principle calls for responsibility in the use of natural resources and awareness of the relationships between humans and the environment. Land is not simply an exploitable resource or a material good; it is a living entity. Land is the *Ñuke Mapu*, the mother that nurtures and protects the community. Maintaining respect and reciprocity is not a mere convention, but an inescapable obligation. This attitude reflects a way of understanding life and our connection to the world.

Ngen mapu demands responsible management of natural resources that keeps future generations in mind. The *Lafkenche* and *Wenteche* communities, for example, have developed land use practices that respect natural cycles, adapt to biodiversity, and preserve the health of the territory. Traditional agricultural methods, passed down from generation to generation, reflect this accumulated knowledge and the ability to observe nature's cycles, so human interventions do not upset the balance of the *mapu*. Thus, the *ngen mapu* guides practical actions that honor the forces and rhythms that sustain life.

The ethics of *ngen mapu* require that everyone in the community assume clear and shared responsibilities for preserving the *mapu*. The land is not the exclusive property of any individual: it belongs to everyone. Any undermining of its integrity affects the community as a whole. This responsibility is transmitted from generation to generation through collective knowledge called *kom kimün*, which encompasses both respect for nature and fundamental knowledge of traditional medicine, social organization, and agriculture.

Norche is a fundamental ethic that refers to the state of equilibrium that should be maintained in all relationships, both human and natural. *Norche* is more than a respectful attitude; it is a principle of regulation that ensures harmony. Every relationship should be based on moderation and mutual respect to maintain balance. This ethical value seeks to avoid conflict and promote reconciliation through dialogue and cooperation. By understanding *norche* as a fundamental mandate, the community is organized around the idea that individual actions should be aligned with collective welfare.

Respect and reciprocity are key aspects of *norche*, which dictate that community life be based on collaboration and mutual assistance. This is manifested in practices such as *rukache*, which is the construction of collective housing, and *minga*, which refers to collaborative agricultural work. All members of the community feel they are part of a whole and protected. In conflict resolution, *norche* demands that differences be overcome through dialogue and mediation, avoiding direct confrontations that could threaten balance and community cohesion. Thus, the search for peace and cooperation is an essential foundation for group's stability and continuity.

Reciprocity is also a central value in the family context, reflected in the respect toward the elders, who occupy a preeminent place in Mapuche social structure. The elders transmit traditions and ancestral knowledge, sustain collective memory, and are a direct link with past generations. Caring for the elderly is not optional; it is a duty that ensures cultural continuity and intergenerational learning. Abandoning them would be considered a serious fault that would break the cycle of reciprocity and weaken community cohesion and integrity. In this sense, reciprocity is more than material exchange; it is a long-term commitment to shared well-being and preservation of cultural identity.

This ethical system sees the individual as a component of a larger whole in which every action has consequences and in which every being occupies a specific place. The *admapu* is the normative framework that guides interactions. This set of norms is not a rigid system of laws but a code of ethics and conduct that guarantees respect and harmony in all aspects of life. Unlike other codes of conduct, it includes relationship with nature, community coexistence, and the rules for collective decision-making. Each member of Mapuche society commits to complying with the *admapu*, recognizing that social balance and peace depend on observing these principles.

Mapuche ethics are a form of cultural resistance that preserves their identity in the face of historical adversities. Defending territory, maintaining customs, and transmitting ethical values to the next generation ensure their community integrity. Every act of cultural preservation is an expression of a profound commitment to balance, reciprocity, and the continuity of their worldview in a changing world.

CHAPTER 2

SACRED NATURE IN MAPUCHE CULTURE

The natural environment as an expression of the sacred

The Mapuche worldview addresses the intricate connections between natural elements and their manifestations. This perspective conceives each component of the world as a bearer of meanings and powers that sustain the harmony of the cosmos. Mountains, rivers, forests, lakes, and the fundamental elements—water, earth, wind, and fire—are living forces that exert a direct influence on the community and the universal balance.

Each element and place are part of a system of interrelationships. Human beings are just one of the participants; they do not have unilateral dominance over the other components. The interaction between humans and nature is based on respect and a sense of reciprocity that fosters harmonious coexistence. This means that nature is not conceived solely as a resource at the disposal of human needs, but as a set of entities and forces whose integrity must be preserved, for human benefit and as a moral duty.

Some places carry particular powers or energies and are considered sacred. At these sites, the boundaries between the visible and invisible worlds are more permeable, allowing for communication between people and forces that protect and guide life. Sacred places are respected and cared for, since any unwise intervention could trigger consequences and disrupt the cosmic order.

Chapter 2: Sacred nature in Mapuche culture

The mountains are centers of connection with the transcendent, acting as guardians of ancestral wisdom and mediators between humanity and the forces that govern the universe. Their summits symbolize rootedness and permanence, reaffirming the cultural identity and collective memory of the Mapuche people. The *machis*—authorities in matters of ceremony and healing—ascend these heights to perform rituals and to seek guidance and strength. The ceremonies express reverence toward these living mountains, honoring their energies and preserving their spiritual power intact. On the Lanín and Llaima volcanoes, for instance, people gain access to vast knowledge and receive protection from the entities that dwell within them.

Rivers represent the flow of life and continuous rebirth. They connect the community's past and present with its traditions and ancestors. They are not regarded merely as bodies of water with utilitarian value, but as living entities endowed with a vital force known as *newen*. *Newen* signifies strength, energy, or spirit—an animating power that transforms rivers into channels of communication with past generations and spaces of purification and renewal. Rivers connect community memory and the forces that have shaped its history. Aware of the importance of rivers for the continuity of life and collective health, the Mapuche treat them with respect and responsibility. They do not alter their course or pollute them, as this would constitute a transgression against the very essence of life.

The forest is where nature's protective energies and regenerative forces converge. Trees, especially the canelo, guard the knowledge and health of the community. The canelo forms a living bond between the different worlds, and its presence is indispensable in rituals that seek peace and balance. The forest provides *machis* with medicinal plants. They do not collect plants indiscriminately but follow guidelines that ensure the health of the ecosystem, since each plant possesses a load of knowledge and energy that should not be depleted. The conservation ethic that unfolds reflects an understanding of the healing properties of plants as well as a willingness to preserve the forest as a place of learning and as a sanctuary of life.

Lakes, with their stillness and depth, are also revered as places of mystery and communion with the unknown. These bodies of water are gateways to other dimensions and harbor energies that are not always evident but can manifest themselves in symbolic ways. Some lakes harbor energies that can send messages or warnings to those who can interpret them. Ceremonies for honoring lake spirits seek harmony, peaceful coexistence, and mutual respect between the inhabitants of the land and the forces that dwell in the water. Maintaining the purity and tranquility of the lakes thus becomes a collective commitment, since any action that disturbs lake waters can trigger a loss of balance in the ecosystem.

The Mapuche relationships with the elements— water, earth, wind, and fire—reveal another dimension of their worldview. Every element plays a specific role in the cycle of life and in maintaining universal harmony. These elements are present on the physical plane. They have their own characteristics that require respect and caution. Thus, interaction with them is carefully regulated and symbolized through acts of communion that seek to honor and preserve the natural balance.

Water is valued as an indispensable resource for life and a purifying force that connects the visible plane with subtler spheres of reality. Rituals involving water seek to renew the bond between human beings and the vital energy that surrounds us. Altering the natural course of water is considered disrespectful to the laws that govern the cosmic order; therefore, the Mapuche strive to preserve water sources as a way of keeping this sacred bond with nature intact.

The earth, known in Mapudungun as *mapu*, is the mother and origin of all existence. This conception goes far beyond a simple reference to the soil or the earth's surface; *mapu* represents the sustenance of life and the space in which all interactions between living beings take place. In this sense, the land is also the place where the ancestors rest and where the memory of the community is preserved, making every interaction into an act of respect toward those who have come before. The relationship with the land is articulated in a series of responsibilities and commitments, where each activity—from cultivation to construction—is carried out in a way that does not damage its integrity. Thus, gratitude and reciprocity guide every action, giving back to the earth what has been taken, and ensure its future capacity to sustain life.

The wind is the breath of the spirits and a means of communication between the forces of nature. The Mapuche interpret changes in its intensity and direction as environmental signals that can have important meanings for the community. The understanding of the wind as a messenger reinforces the idea that the natural world is in constant communication with human beings and that every change in the environment must be observed and respected.

Finally, fire is an element of transformation. Beyond its everyday uses, it is a means of communication with protective forces and ancestors. In healing rituals, fire creates connections that transcend material experience. Since fire can destroy and regenerate, it symbolizes the end and beginning of cycles; for this reason, the Mapuche use it in ceremonies of purification and harmonization with the energies that govern the universe. Hence, the handling of ritual fires requires particular sensitivity, and its use must be accompanied by an attitude of respect for the duality of their nature.

The *ngen*: guardian spirits of nature

Entities called *ngen* regulate and protect natural elements. These immaterial guardians observe and ensure balance and sustainability. They are symbolic authorities that connect humans and nature by fostering reciprocity and mutual respect. Each *ngen* has its domain, such as land, water, or mountains, and regulates human behavior with respect to resources, thus establishing an ethical system that is central to Mapuche culture.

The *ngen mapu*, protector of the land, preserves the physical elements and the vitality of the environment. The land is an entity with consciousness and rights. The *ngen mapu* guarantees the fertility and well-being of all beings that depend on it. This guardian establishes the need for an ethical use of resources and demands that any intervention, such as planting or harvesting, be carried out with respect and permission. The land is treated as a dignified being that must be honored.

To obtain the approval of the *ngen mapu*, the Mapuche perform ceremonies before disturbing the soil. These rituals seek a connection with the land and honor its role in sustaining, ensuring that the balance maintained by the *ngen mapu* is not affected by human activities. They are a tangible expression of respect that manifests a commitment to preserving its richness and vitality for future generations. The *ngen mapu* reinforces the belief in an intrinsic reciprocity between humans and nature.

Fresh water is under the guardianship of the *ngen ko*. Water is an essential daily resource that also fosters communal union with the transcendental. The *ngen ko* ensures its the purity and availability. Bodies of water must remain unaltered and protected from destruction. The Mapuche express their respect for the *ngen ko* by placing offerings in rivers and lakes before using them, thus expressing their gratitude and ethical commitment to water conservation. This perspective conceives of water as a dignified entity.

In coastal areas and in the sea, the *ngen lafken* is the guardian in charge of salt waters and marine ecosystems. The *lafken* is much more than a physical space; it is a powerful and mysterious dimension that requires a prudent and respectful relationship. Unlike other natural environments, the sea is perceived as an autonomous realm, filled with unpredictable forces. Interaction with the sea involves ceremonies and offerings that ask the *ngen lafken* for protection and permission to use marine resources.

Mountains are guarded by the *ngen wingkul*, who watches over their sacredness and integrity. Mountains are for retreat and contemplation, conducive to introspection and connection with the ineffable. The *ngen wingkul* manifests itself through natural phenomena, such as wind or storms, which are interpreted as messages that remind them of the respect that these elevated spaces deserve. Hunting and gathering in the mountains require the authorization of the *ngen wingkul*, who ensures that these activities do not disturb mountain balance.

Interacting with the *ngen* requires responsibility and reciprocity. These guardians protect and place limits on activities in their domains. Actions must be humane and respectful, avoiding any form of abuse or exploitation that could have negative consequences for the natural balance or social cohesion. Any violation against a *ngen*, such as polluting water or over-using natural resources, affects the order of the natural world and the harmony and well-being of the community. The Mapuche recognize that in order to maintain a harmonious coexistence, every interaction with the environment must be carried out with the consent and blessing of the *ngen*.

The *ngen* structure is a worldview that goes beyond protecting natural resources. They embody a system of meanings that places human beings in a position of interdependence with the environment, reminding them of their responsibility to preserve nature. They consolidate a vision in which the survival and well-being of humanity depends on its ability to coexist in harmony with the forces that govern the natural world.

Animals as symbols and spiritual guides

Animals also participate in the network of meanings that connect the visible and invisible. They inhabit the natural environment but they also fulfill functions of mediation and symbolization. They have a specific place in the Mapuche understanding of the universe and constitute a manifestation of natural forces. They are a repository of fundamental teachings. In their interactions with animals, the Mapuche find qualities to emulate and ways to unravel the connections between the human being and the totality of the cosmos.

The condor, the puma, and the fox appear in ancient myths. These myths teach introspection, resilience, and how to integrate into an interdependent environment. Through them, the Mapuche explore the connection between nature and human beings, as well as access to dimensions beyond the ordinary senses.

The condor, or *mallku*, is a sacred being that crosses earthly spaces and other planes, linking heaven and earth. *Mallkus* soar higher than any other animal. They symbolize the search for knowledge with a broad and deep look at reality. In Mapuche mythology, the condor is the guardian of archaic knowledge who protects the secrets passed down from ancestral times and rules the skies of the Andes. Those who manage to establish a connection with the condor acquire a sharper vision of natural balances. They can grasp aspects of reality that would otherwise remain hidden. The presence of a condor is interpreted as a sign of transformation for those who take on roles of responsibility. The condor's flight is a metaphor for rising above circumstances and developing an expanded perception of life.

In dreams, the condor is an omen of profound change, especially for community leaders. Its appearance suggests coming events and offers guidance for crucial decisions. This bird is an emblem of perseverance and strength, representing the ability to overcome obstacles in the material world. Its majestic flight is a symbol of freedom and perspective. By inviting human beings to observe their lives from a higher vantage point, the condor inspires physical strength and self-knowledge. This fosters perspectives that transcend the apparent and calls us to see beyond the limitations imposed by the immediate environment.

The puma, or *pangi*, embodies strength and power. It represents courage and the ability to face adversity. It is associated with the skill and intelligence necessary to survive in difficult environments, making it a symbol of protection in the mountains. Its solitary nature and ability to move undetected make it an emblem of self-sufficiency and determination. A precise and careful hunter, it symbolizes the balance between strength and prudence, ferocity and discernment. In Mapuche stories, the puma often appears as a silent and calculating leader, teaching the importance of careful reflection and acting only when strictly necessary. It is a master of strategy, vigilance, and survival. In dreams, the puma is a call to face imminent challenges with determination; it reminds us to act with integrity and responsibility. Seeing a puma inspires confidence in one's own abilities and the courage to take on challenges, part of an ideal life in which courage and wisdom converge.

The fox, *ngürü*, stands out for its ingenuity and adaptability. It symbolizes the ability to respond to difficult circumstances with creativity and flexibility, demonstrating that intelligence can be a more powerful resource than brute strength. It is valued for its speed and efficiency in solving problems, as well as its ability to survive in adverse situations. Its knowledge of plants and hidden paths allows it to endure times of scarcity. In traditional tales, it overcomes its enemies through trickery or cunning. One of the most popular fox stories is about a fox convincing a hunter that he brings a message of good fortune. This shows that the fox's true power lies in overcoming dangers through intelligence and prudence. Mental acuity and flexibility are essential attributes for facing the vicissitudes of life. Thus, the fox inspires those who seek to resolve conflicts with ingenuity, adapt to circumstances, and rely on cunning rather than confrontation.

Beyond its role in stories, the fox represents a philosophy of life based on adaptability and resilience. It is a model of how living beings can harmoniously integrate into their environment and adapt without imposing their will on the natural balance. In dreams, it reminds us that mental agility and flexibility can open doors to unexpected solutions, even in the most complex situations.

In Mapuche culture, animals are integrated into a worldview that respects and honors them as beings with a cosmic mission. They are understood as repositories of wisdom that transcends human life, a kind of connection between human beings and the principles that govern reality. Through their presence in stories, myths, and dreams, the condor, the puma, and the fox are role models and guides toward a more fulfilling and conscious life. Their teachings are not transmitted explicitly, but through experiences and observation. They teach courage, adaptability, intelligence, and respect for the environment. They are vehicles of knowledge that connect individuals with the elements that make up the universe. This relationship of reciprocity and reverence toward animals is a matter of tradition and a profound expression of Mapuche ethics, centered on living in balance with the environment and recognizing and thanking each being for its teachings.

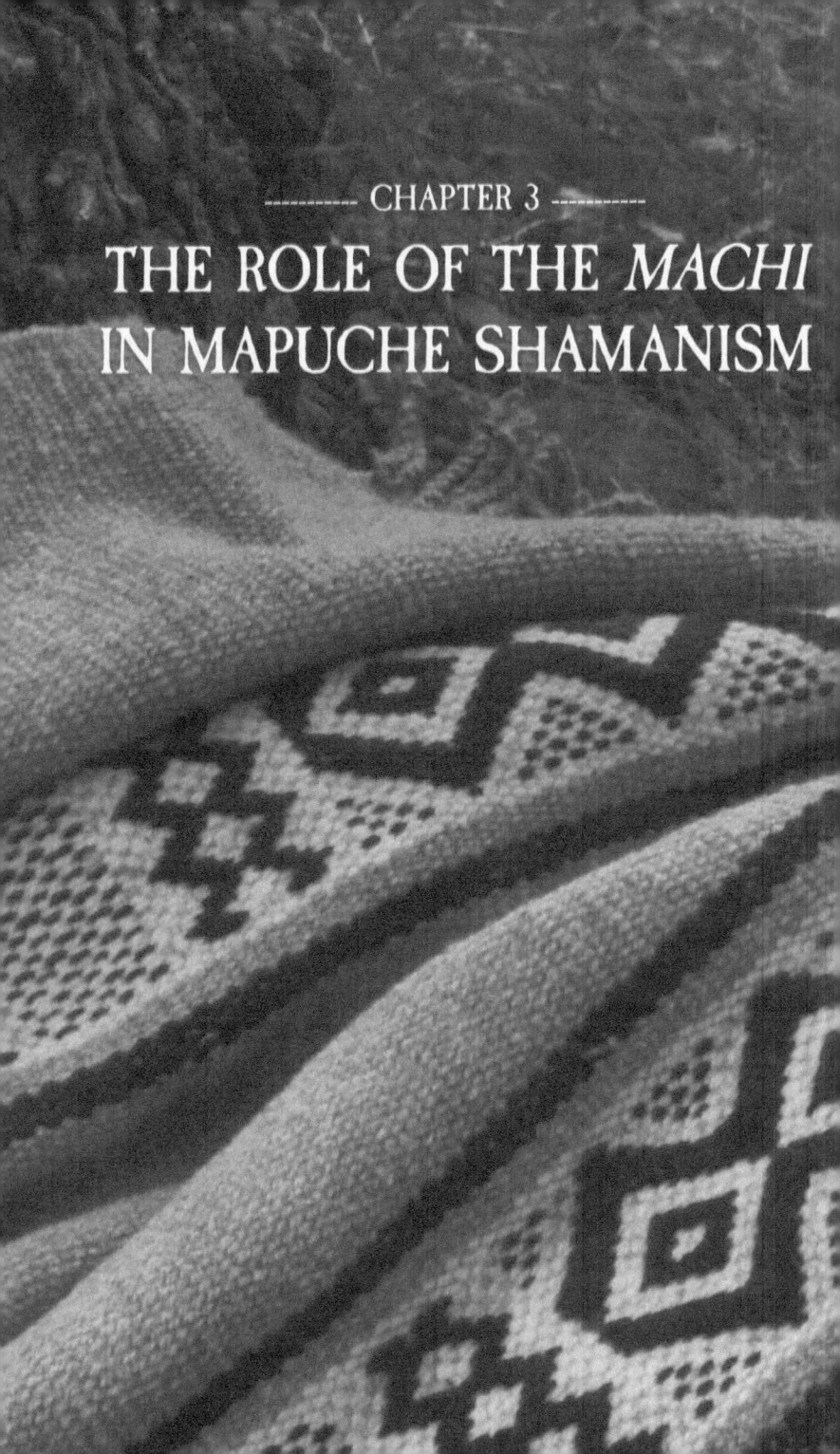

CHAPTER 3
THE ROLE OF THE *MACHI* IN MAPUCHE SHAMANISM

What is a *machi*? Origin and spiritual function

A *machi* is a healer, a ritual leader, and a channel who maintains cohesion among the community and energies that are fundamental for harmony and balance. The *machi* is a reservoir of wisdom and a bridge to invisible forces. Her system of beliefs and practices reflects a worldview in which nature and its manifestations are living, sacred entities. A *machi*'s existence and work are sustained by a network of meanings. In this network, each natural element possesses its own essence, and human beings are called to live in harmony with the forces that surround them.

Machis are usually identified in childhood, in girls who show an unusual sensitivity to the natural world and its unseen energies. This can be revealed in dreams, visions, or a natural inclination toward healing and service to others. These signs are interpreted as a call from a *wengkufe*, an invisible protector who establishes a special bond with the chosen girl. That initial bond marks the beginning of an extensive training process involving years of discipline, sacrifice, and dedication to develop the skills and knowledge required for the work of a *machi*. The future *machi* undergoes a series of teachings ranging from the study of medicinal plants to the rituals necessary to communicate with the forces of nature. Guided by an experienced *machi*, the apprentice faces tests of physical endurance as well as empathy and commitment to community well-being. This learning process is rigorous and continuous, focused on developing the skills necessary to interpret messages from invisible energies and perform ceremonies that restore harmony when it is threatened. Through introspection, self-control, and constant contact with nature, a *machi* learns to perceive that which escapes the common person. She acquires practical wisdom and knowledge of human complexity.

One of the most important instruments in *machis'* work is the *rewe*, a symbolic wooden structure that represents an intersection between the earthly plane and higher dimensions. The *rewe* is a sacred pillar through which offerings and prayers are channeled and allows a *machi* to establish a connection with invisible energies and facilitate communication. Around the *rewe*, the community gathers to witness healing rituals, celebrations, and rites of passage that consolidate the sense of unity and belonging. In this context, the *machi* is not an individual endowed with personal powers, but rather an intermediary who acts in accordance with the will of nature and the forces that sustain her.

As healer, the *machi*'s role goes beyond the physical realm, since illness is understood as a manifestation of imbalances between an individual and the environment and its energies. Hence, *machis* adopt a holistic approach that addresses physical, emotional, and elements that may be involved in the patient's discomfort. Rituals such as the *machi kutran* invoke invisible forces and restore harmony. The *machi*'s sensitivity and perception play a crucial role in identifying the origin of evil and acting on it.

Machis' power of interpretation makes them essential figures in community life. Their ability to receive visions and anticipate events allows them to guide others. Their dreams and visions are messages of warning or guidance sent by higher forces, so they are leaders in times of uncertainty.

Through stories, teachings, and rituals, *machis* educate young people in the values and traditions that shape Mapuche identity, ensuring that the knowledge accumulated over centuries continues in future generations. This function is essential for maintaining cultural cohesion and for ensuring that Mapuche wisdom remains relevant in a constantly changing world.

Machis play a fundamental role in rites of passage, especially in ceremonies that accompany the deceased on their journey to the world of the ancestors. They lead prayers and chants to guide the spirit to its new state, ensuring that it finds peace and harmony. This links them directly to the world of ancestors, protectors, and invisible guides of the community. Such rituals keep the bond with ancestors alive, remind the community of the importance of honoring and respecting those who have departed and ensure that their legacy continues to influence everyday life.

Machis also connect with the energies that inhabit nature, such as mountains, rivers, and forests, to which they attribute their own qualities and wills. Bonds of respect and reciprocity must be woven with these living forces. They maintain a constant dialogue with these entities through rituals and offerings, requesting their support and thanking them for their presence in community life. This bond is essential to preserving harmony and preventing nature from being altered or damaged by irresponsible human actions.

Machis influence every aspect of community life, from healing and spiritual guidance to teaching and environmental protection. They are role models of dedication and service, and figures of authority. They do not impose their own power: they collaborate with higher forces. Their work bears witness to the ancestral wisdom and worldview of the Mapuche, who conceive of human life as an inseparable part of a larger system.

Machis adapt and transform in response to the challenges facing the community, integrating ancestral traditions with current needs. This dynamism allows them to keep Mapuche traditions alive and, at the same time, strengthen their culture in the face of external influences and the pressures of modernity, which threaten the survival of their beliefs. Ultimately, the *machis* represent the resilience of cultural practices and indigenous wisdom, vital sources of knowledge and guidance in the contemporary world.

The initiation ceremony: the *machitun*

The *machitun* is a public ceremony that consecrates a *machi*. It is a process of community integration and validation that consolidates the *machi*'s role as mediator between the community and the forces of nature. The ceremony confers authority and confirms her ability to act as a guide and protector of the cosmic balance. It publicly recognizes her extensive training, which has endowed her with healing powers and the ability to interpret signs. In this way, the *machitun* is the culmination of a training path that has prepared the aspirant to channel new skills and ancestral wisdom in the service of the community. This requires a connection with nature, its cycles, and its dynamics, as well as a sensitivity to read the meaning of dreams and other symbols.

The *machitun* reflects and celebrates the indissoluble link between human beings and universal forces and, in this sense, renews the bonds that sustain the natural order and collective well-being. The ceremony transforms the *machi* into a respected figure and a medium between the community and the energies that are perceived as sources of life and health. One of the essential elements is the *rewe*, a wooden object considered a cosmic axis, which allows symbolic contact between the human world and the world of unseen forces. Before it, the aspiring *machi* bows with reverence, surrender, and respect in order to accept higher energies.

To prepare the *machitún*, an appropriate space is selected. It should be close to nature, to enable uninterrupted communication with the energies of the earth. This space is carefully prepared so that all elements favor natural connections. The community and attendees fast and make offerings to establish an atmosphere of respect and purification and to give the ceremony the solemnity it deserves. Thus, participants assume an attitude of contemplation while performing rituals that facilitate the transition to a state of purity. Together, this creates an atmosphere of deep respect for the *machi* and the forces invoked in the rite.

The *rewe* is adorned with offerings that represent the commitment of the community and the *machi* to remain in harmony with natural energies. The *rewe* becomes a channel, a point of convergence between the higher forces and the community's desire to receive their favors and protection.

Food and drink are essential offerings, carefully selected and arranged around the *rewe*. They express gratitude and acknowledge the authority of the forces of nature. Medicinal herbs and plants purify and legitimize traditional medicinal knowledge. Herbs create an environment conducive to trance and communion with the invisible and reinforce the *machi*'s commitment to the healing knowledge inherited from previous generations. Every detail, every offering, and every symbol adds a layer of meaning, confirming the *machi*'s role as protector of traditional knowledge and the spiritual integrity of the community.

An essential part of the *machitun* is the trance entered into by the *machi*, which allows her to communicate deeply with higher forces. This trance is facilitated by ritual songs and dances that focus attention and create conducive conditions. The trance is understood as an authentic union with unseen energies that grant visions and messages of special relevance to the community. These visions strengthen the *machi*'s determination and demonstrate her willingness and aptitude to be a mediator. Through this trance, the *machi* accesses knowledge beyond what is accessible to others, which legitimizes her authority as a guide and counselor.

The *machitun* reaffirms the principles of Mapuche culture, which prioritizes harmony with invisible forces and the environment. Each of the movements and phases of the ceremony is loaded with meaning and reflects the values that sustain community life. At the conclusion, the *machi* is reborn, invested with the authority and legitimacy necessary to be a spiritual leader responsible for the well-being of the community and maintaining balance with nature. This consecration makes her indispensable, a pillar of Mapuche culture. The *machitun* ensures that the *machi* is duly recognized and prepared to perform her role as mediator, healer, and protector for as long as she retains the support of these energies and the respect of those around her. In this way, she becomes a symbol of the reciprocal relationship with the universe.

The healing role of the *machi* and shamanic practices

A *machi*'s work is based on a cosmovision built on a deep connection between health and balance. Healing

Chapter 3: The role of the machi in Mapuche shamanism

addresses physical ailments but encompasses all facets of life, allowing it to address more subtle aspects of existence. In Mapuche thought, the person and the cosmos are in a dynamic and mutual balance, and it is the responsibility of the *machi* to ensure that this order is maintained. This is the purpose of the *machis'* training, which transcends mere teaching. They are part of a tradition of knowledge that is assimilated through direct experience and constant observation, and then passed on to new generations of *machis*.

Machis follow a symbolic code that confers authority and legitimacy through tradition, which acknowledges the respected role of mediator between various forces and planes of existence. This role is reinforced by the use of natural elements that are meticulously employed in ceremonies. Medicinal plants are powerful and symbolic tools, capable of restoring lost balance. They are selected for their healing effects and their connections to natural elements that sustain harmony.

Each plant has an intrinsic symbolism and power and *machis* have knowledge of their preparation and application. These herbs and plants are collected at specific times of the year and in sacred places, as natural cycles play a crucial role in their effectiveness. Gathering plants is not casual; it follows a protocol that guarantees their potency. Any deviation can affect healing, so the process must be respected. In healing ceremonies, the *machi* manipulates plants with ceremonial gestures, words, chants, and prayers that enhance their properties.

These ceremonies are also gatherings since it often involves the entire community. They are much more than a moment of individual healing: they are instances of communion in which cultural ties are strengthened and collective identity is sustained. For the Mapuche people, the illness of one of its members affects the whole, and the healing process restores the balance of the entire group. Healing ceremonies underscore the cohesion and fundamental principles of community life, reminding everyone of their connection to nature and the cosmos.

The *machi* also uses instruments such as the *kultrun*, a drum that symbolizes the Mapuche universe and its cardinal points. The sound of the drum harmonizes the energies of the space and those present. The *kultrun* represents the totality of the cosmos; each beat is a call to restore balance between body, mind, and environment. Its beat is capable of transforming energies and driving away forces that can cause harm or discomfort, helping to activate a healing that transcends the physical.

The guidance of the *machi* continues after the ceremony. Follow-up includes recommendations for maintaining the balance achieved during the ritual. These may include changes in diet or the use of specific plants as amulets. Preserving well-being is a joint effort that requires the participation of the community.

The relationship between the *machi* and the individuals is based on trust and respect for her knowledge, considered a gift passed down through generations.

CHAPTER 3: THE ROLE OF THE MACHI IN MAPUCHE SHAMANISM

Machis' healing work synthesizes the fundamental aspects of the Mapuche cosmovision. Personal and community well-being are part of the same fabric. Each being is deeply connected to their environment, and the balance between forces depends on preserving this sacred interconnection.

CHAPTER 4
FUNDAMENTAL RITES OF MAPUCHE SPIRITUALITY

Ngillatun: the rite of thanks and petition

The *ngillatun* is a ceremony that pays homage to the forces of nature and the protective entities, *ngen*, who watch over universal balance. This ceremony expresses gratitude, requests support at crucial moments, and reinforces collective identity, all framed in an ancestral tradition that emphasizes respect and reciprocity with the environment and its guardians. It is set for a specific time and place, based on natural cycles, so it aligns with the harmony of the earth and the cosmos.

This community-centered ceremony strengthens internal bonds and reaffirms shared values. Organizing the ritual is laborious and requires the collaboration and participation of all members of the community. The ceremony is led by *lonkos* and *machis*, custodians of ancestral knowledge, gifted with a special sensitivity to interpret natural signs, as well as the ability to guide the group in performing the ceremony.

The prayers and chants are performed in Mapudungun, the Mapuche language in which each word carries an intrinsic power that facilitates communication with the *ngen*. Correct pronunciation and intonation are vital for the messages to be fully understood, as language is a direct vehicle for transmitting intention and respect.

The chants, *ül*, are a central part of the *ngillatun*. They invoke natural energies and unify community members in a shared vibration. The ceremonial drum called *kultrun* sets the rhythm. It guides the community dance and reinforces cohesion. The dance is performed in a circle around the *rewe* and represents unity. Participants set aside their individuality to integrate into the whole in an act of cosmic communion.

Offerings are also important, including traditional foods such as *muday*, a drink made from fermented corn, as well as breads, fruits, and other products of the land, which are arranged around the *rewe* to symbolize gratitude. The order in which the offerings are placed responds to ancestral knowledge that honors and respects the cosmological principles.

The *ngillatun* reaffirms community cohesion and healing. In times of internal conflict or individual tensions, it offers a space for reconciliation and restoration of balance and harmony. The elders, in particular, contribute their wisdom and experience to this process, evoking past ceremonies and contextualizing traditional values and teachings. The youth absorb and learn these values, ensuring cultural continuity from generation to generation.

The *ngillatun* manifests respect for the natural environment and symbolizes the connection between human beings and nature. The well-being of the community is understood as a reflection of the health of the land. In this way, the *ngillatun* reaffirms the Mapuche responsibility for ecological balance and a relationship with nature governed by respect and continuous care.

During the *ngillatun*, requests are made for the fertility of the land, the well-being of community members, protection from adversity, and prosperity in general. These petitions are made with an attitude of humility that recognizes the autonomy of these entities. The *ngen* are free to respond according to the natural order, and the community accepts their will as part of the process of coexistence and mutual respect.

In agricultural work, the Mapuche perform gratitude ceremonies and ask permission from the spirits of the earth before harvesting. This reflects a reverence for the environment, as they believe that the spirits of their ancestors inhabit nature and act as protectors of human activities. Farmers believe that these spirits help maintain ecological balance, ensuring soil fertility for future generations and promoting respectful interaction with the environment.

We tripantu: celebrating the new cycle

The celebration of *We tripantu*, the "birth of a new sun," symbolizes changing seasons and crystallizes profound ideas about cyclical renewal and cosmic balance. Every year, it renews the sacred relationship between humans, nature, and the forces that balance the universe. It takes place around the winter solstice in the southern hemisphere, approximately June 21. It marks the culmination of one annual cycle and the opening of another, thus manifesting a conception of time radically different from the linear vision of Western cultures. In Mapuche thought, time is not a cumulative succession of events, but a circular return to the principles of unity and harmony that link living beings and all elements of creation.

We tripantu alludes to the rebirth of both the earth and the energies that animate all beings. This annual transformation signals a change in the length of days and opens the door to a process of spiritual and physical renewal. The ceremony celebrates the beginning of a new cycle of life that unfolds in the gradual increase of light, symbolizing the resurgence of life itself and the regeneration of the bonds of interdependence that sustain the Mapuche world. The return of the sun is more than a natural phenomenon; it is an occasion to restore and strengthen the natural environment and community ties that constitute the essence of Mapuche culture.

One of the fundamental principles of *We tripantu* is reciprocity and respect for the forces of nature. All elements—water, wind, flora, and fauna—are vital to the continuity of existence. Participants release the impurities accumulated during the year and prepare for a renewed state of personal and collective balance.

Preparations begin days before the main ceremony and involve all members of the community, in order to synchronize the energies of each participant with the new cycle. This includes everything from a thorough cleaning of domestic and community spaces to preparing offerings and special foods. Food preparation represents coming abundance in the new cycle and expresses gratitude for the bounty of the previous cycle.

The main ceremony takes place at dawn, in an outdoor space carefully chosen for its connection to nature. There, the community gathers around a bonfire that symbolizes the warmth of life and the energy that is reborn after the phase of darkness. The bonfire is the center of the celebration and represents the vital energy that will accompany the participants in the new cycle. Rituals include songs, dances, and prayers that express unity and respect toward the forces that protect and sustain the cosmic order.

Among the central rituals of *We tripantu* is purification through water, an element laden with symbolism in Mapuche culture. Community members approach a river, lake, or spring and are sprinkled or immersed in cold water to symbolize regeneration and the beginning of a new cycle. This ritual recognizes water as a vital element and source of renewal. For the Mapuche people, the waters of rivers and lakes possess a special power that purifies both body and spirit, allowing each person to enter the new cycle with renewed energy.

The *We tripantu* ceremony provides an opportunity for introspection and reconciliation, allowing people to reflect on the past year, resolve outstanding conflicts, and commit to new resolutions that benefit both the community and nature. This concerns individuals and families and reinforces a sense of belonging and social cohesion. Renewed resolutions allow the Mapuche people to reaffirm the principles of interdependence and mutual respect that underpin their worldview.

Dancing and singing are essential aspects of the *We tripantu*. Community dances express gratitude to the forces of nature. Chants invoke protective entities. The dances are performed in a circle around the bonfire. The drum sets the rhythm of the celebration, and its sound is perceived as a deep bond between the participants and the natural environment.

For the Mapuche people, human beings are part of a greater whole, and *We tripantu* serves as a reminder of the responsibility of each individual and the community to preserve cosmic balance.

The *lof* as the center of ceremonial life

The *lof* is a fundamental social group that articulates a network of cultural and kinship relationships. *Lofs* are family groups united by shared blood ties and constitute the core of Mapuche collective identity.

Lofs are organized around extended family units that share a common cultural identity and a shared worldview, nourished by a series of ceremonies and rituals performed together. Each member of the community plays a specific role oriented toward collective well-being, especially in the ritual sphere. *Lofs* allow the community to maintain balance and adapt to external changes without losing its identity or essential values.

The *machi*, the *lonko*, and the elders are key figures in a *lof*. The *machi* mediates between the members of the *lof* and the natural environment in ritual contexts and in the resolution of internal conflicts. Through her medicinal knowledge, she symbolizes the essential connection between the *lof* and the environment, ensuring the physical and emotional health of the community while preserving traditional healing knowledge.

The *lonko* plays a leadership role based on respect and his ability to guide the community according to tradition and ethical principles. His authority extends to the social, political, and ceremonial spheres and is essential for preserving the norms and values that organize daily life and ritual development in the *lof*.

The *lof* organizes ceremonies throughout the year that strengthen social cohesion and links with the forces of nature. Celebrations may request protection or offer thanks for harvests or for peace after conflict.

The concept of *küme mogen*, or "good life," is a guiding principle that prioritizes collective well-being over individual interests. In practice, *küme mogen* suggests a conscious and balanced use of natural resources that promotes harmonious coexistence between people and the environment. This principle is reflected in all activities, from farming to gathering wild plants, and represents an understanding of the interdependence between human beings and the cosmos.

Daily life in the *lof* is marked by a series of gestures and symbolic actions that show respect for the natural balance, for example, when gathering medicinal plants. This ethic extends to activities such as hunting and fishing, which are preceded by rituals aimed at minimizing the impact on the ecosystem and paying homage to the life that is taken.

CHAPTER 5

SHAMANIC PRACTICES AND SPIRITUAL HEALING

The practice of *lawen*: medicinal plants in rituals

Mapuche herbal medicine, known in Mapudungun as *lawen*, is a system that channels and honors the energies of the earth. Each plant has an intrinsic force that connects with the cosmic energies and holistically harmonizes body and spirit. *Lawen* has therapeutic benefits as well as a ritual and symbolic dimension. Respect, balance, and veneration for nature are fundamental.

Lawen knowledge is passed down from generation to generation, usually under the tutelage of the *machi*. It includes the healing properties of each plant, its growth cycles, the right time for harvesting, and how to use it to treat ailments.

This knowledge integrates technical details with holistic wisdom, making the *machis* bridges between the community and natural energies at every stage of the process, from harvesting to treatment in ceremonial contexts.

The set of herbs that make up the *lawen* is extensive and carefully selected to treat a variety of conditions, both physical and emotional. Among them are those from the canelo (*Drimys winteri*), a tree sacred to the Mapuche culture, which serve as analgesics, anti-inflammatories, and antipyretics. It is also used in ceremonies to summon protective energies. It heals the body and provides stability and security to those who participate in its rituals. Another essential plant is boldo (*Peumus boldus*), widely recognized for its beneficial effects on the digestive system and its ability to restore emotional balance. It also has community value, as it is used in ceremonies that promote social cohesion and mutual respect. Likewise, matico (*Buddleja globosa*) is known for its antiseptic and healing properties and is used to treat wounds and respiratory problems. Quillay (*Quillaja saponaria*) is used for its expectorant and anti-inflammatory effects, with benefits for the respiratory system. In purification ceremonies, quillay is used for its symbolic ability to renew and revitalize the body and spirit, evoking cleanliness and rebirth. Paico (*Chenopodium ambrosioides*) is beneficial for the digestive system and can help fight parasitic infections. The use of these plants reflects the meticulous observation of nature that characterizes the Mapuche knowledge system.

Gathering medicinal plants involves ethical principles and rituals that express a deep respect toward natural cycles. Harvest times are determined according to the phases of the moon, the season of the year, and the physical and mental state of the *machi*. This respect toward the environment translates into specific gestures and rituals, such as asking the plant for permission before cutting it and offering it a gift of gratitude. These plants are vital elements, and the *machi* establishes a relationship of mutual consideration and care. Harvesting is usually a community activity: those who want to learn *lawen* accompany the *machi*. This transmission of knowledge ensures that future generations will preserve the tradition of *lawen*. At the same time, harvesting is a shared learning experience that strengthens the community and the sense of belonging.

There are specific preparations for each plant that require detailed knowledge at each stage of the process. Depending on the ailment, preparations may include infusions, poultices, ointments, and ritual baths, each with a particular function. All of this enhances the healing properties of each plant. Sometimes, the *machi* may chant or recite prayers to reinforce the efficacy of the treatment, establishing a connection between the sick person and the natural healing forces. The treatments require active participation and an open and receptive attitude. The interaction between the individual and the *machi* requires trust and respect for her ancestral knowledge. This bond allows the healing process to restore awareness of community belonging and respect for the environment.

As a healer and an authority on medicine, the *machi* regulates the use of remedies to avoid overharvesting plants or using them irresponsibly. Plant extraction follows strict rules of moderation that seek to protect the ecosystem and preserve natural resources for future generations. This ethical management of resources underscores the commitment of the *machi* and the community to sustainability and respect for the life cycle of each plant. *Lawen* is notable for its efficacy and respect for natural resources. Healing is a shared responsibility between the patient, the *machi*, and the community.

Each treatment is a restorative process that allows individuals to regain their place in the network of relationships that constitute the social and ecological structure of the *lof*. Through this system of knowledge, Mapuche herbal medicine has remained a living tradition that responds to health needs and manifests cultural identity and ties to nature.

Spiritual connection in healing: interventions by the *machi*

The *machi*'s role goes beyond medicine; she is an intermediary with powers that escape everyday perception. This capacity allows her to identify and correct imbalances that affect the health and well-being of the community and the individual, restoring a holistic harmony that includes physical, emotional, and energetic aspects.

For the Mapuche people, illness is both a physical and relational imbalance with respect to the environment. This imbalance can have multiple causes, from emotional conflicts to external influences. Hence healing goes beyond visible symptoms and addresses their hidden roots. Treatments employ medicinal plants, ritual ceremonies, and altered states of consciousness, which are key to identifying the underlying causes.

Shamanic trance, essential in the *machi*'s healing practice, is a sophisticated technique for overcoming the limits of ordinary perception and accessing broader realities. This altered state of consciousness gives the *machi* a privileged perspective on the patient's illness, in order to unravel the factors that contribute to the discomfort, both material and intangible. This skill requires knowledge of trance-inducing methods, such as the use of sacred instruments like the *kultrun*.

This drum establishes a direct connection with the forces that govern the natural order, whose influence is essential in the healing process. The *machi* receives visions that reveal the origins of the ailment and the disruptive energies, so that she can apply a treatment based on a holistic understanding of the person. The *machi* assesses the patient's overall situation: their emotional state, their relationship with the community, and the state of their connection with nature. Treatment is aimed at restoring overall balance.

Machis guide patients in self-discovery and transformation, promoting change that goes beyond mere physical recovery. This requires an active involvement of the patient, who must take responsibility for life changes that will help restore balance and avoid ailments. Health is a conscious integration of the individual and the natural order. Patients must understand that healing involves harmony with their environment and with themselves. Individual imbalances are a community problem, so active healing strengthens the social fabric and fosters community cohesion. This reintegrates individuals into a network of interdependence and mutual respect.

Dreams are messages sent by invisible powers, and the *machis* use them to diagnose imbalances. Through dreams, they can identify latent conflicts and dangers and help patients recognize root causes of discomfort. Dream messages can reveal patterns of behavior or circumstances that require attention and change, facilitating healing. Dream interpretation complements trances, providing additional insight that allows *machis* to guide patients toward personal and collective balance. Healing, in this sense, is an act of reconnection with the universe, where every element—from plants to ceremonial rhythms—is interrelated in a system of symbolic correspondences.

The power of chanting and sound in Mapuche spirituality

In Mapuche culture, traditional songs and instruments occupy a preeminent place. Sound is part of ceremonies and also provides access to realities beyond those perceived in an ordinary state. Musical instruments are not ornaments: they are vehicles for interaction between community members and dimensions that escape direct observation. Certain vibrations are essential for achieving balance in the natural and spiritual realms. Each sound contributes to establishing transcendent connections.

Machis uses specific chants to invoke forces of protection and healing. The melodies and rhythms produce specific effects on both the environment and the participants. Each song serves a specific purpose, so that singing becomes a form of knowingness and connection with deeper realities.

In healing rituals, chants allow *machis* to enter altered states of perception, in which it becomes possible to acquire information that would otherwise be inaccessible. In these contexts, singing is a channel for accessing expanded planes of knowingness. Each sound must be executed with precision and respect, as it constitutes an invocation that requires experience and sensitivity. *Machis* must be trained to properly intone each *ül*, allowing them to interact with forces that demand reverence. They adjust the cadence and tone to the specific needs of each ritual, creating a dynamic interaction with the energetic context of the ceremony. This flexible and adaptable nature of the *ül* reflects the Mapuche view of life as a fluid system in constant transformation, in which each action is adapted to the particular situation of the community.

Traditional instruments are imbued with symbolism intertwined with the cosmic structure of the universe. *Machis* beat *kultruns* to connect the visible and invisible planes, using the rhythmic pulse to attract benevolent energies and prepare their minds and bodies to perceive forces that affect the well-being of the community.

The manufacture of *kultruns* follows rules that reflect the integration between humanity and nature. The wood comes from a tree whose strength symbolizes the interdependence of the elements. The animal leather that covers it recognizes the cycle of life and death. The drawings on the membrane represent the essential elements of the worldview—earth, water, air, and fire—

as well as the forces that inhabit each cardinal direction. The geometric design of the drum seeks to attract certain energies and align the ceremony with natural balance.

The sound of the *kultrun* acts as an extension of the *machi*'s energy, who imprints the drum with the appropriate cadence for each occasion and creates a symbiotic relationship with the instrument. Attendees perceive this rhythm as an invitation to enter a state of concentration and receptivity, tuning their individual energies to the collective vibration. The synchronicity strengthens the connections with the invoked forces and creates an environment where energy flows freely between attendees and the environment.

Another important instrument is the *trutruka*, a long trumpet made of cane and horn. It emits a powerful sound that carries over great distances. Its resonance summons the entire community, the forces of nature, and ancestral spirits, reinforcing the sense of belonging and continuity within the Mapuche tradition. The deep, penetrating tone of the *trutruka* evokes respect, consolidates community cohesion, and reaffirms relationships with the elements of nature, considered allies and protectors.

The *pifilca* is a small whistle made of wood or bone. Its high-pitched tone can pierce perceptual barriers and summon protective energies. At key moments in ceremonies, it activates a state of alertness among participants and helps them align with subtle planes of existence.

Each instrument and each sound has a unique resonance that suits the nature of the ritual. *Machis* are connoisseurs of these properties, so they can select the best-suited instruments for the occasion. These choices are based on detailed knowledge of the instruments' vibrations and symbolic properties, so that each ceremony is constructed as an architecture of energy and sound.

Group singing complements the individual sounds of each instrument, reinforcing the sense of belonging. Each individual, by participating in the chant, brings his or her energy and connects with the collective, amplifying the effect of the ritual. The vibration of the voices in unison allows the community to operate as a single entity that strengthens the bond with the invoked dimensions.

Singing and sound are means of communication with forces beyond the realm of ordinary senses. Both the individual chants of the *machi* and the resonances of the instruments enable interaction with realities that would otherwise remain hidden. These ceremonies maintain a continuous relationship with the ancestors and with the forces that guarantee order and continuity of life in the universe, where every sound and every rhythm is considered an expression of an interconnected web that sustains the world.

Music becomes a language that transcends words and paves the way for universal balance. Sounds have the ability to restore harmony and connect human beings with the forces that govern their existence, establishing a flow of life and energy that ensures the continuity of their cultural identity and their relationship with the natural environment.

CHAPTER 6
THE CONNECTION WITH THE AFTERLIFE IN MAPUCHE SPIRITUALITY

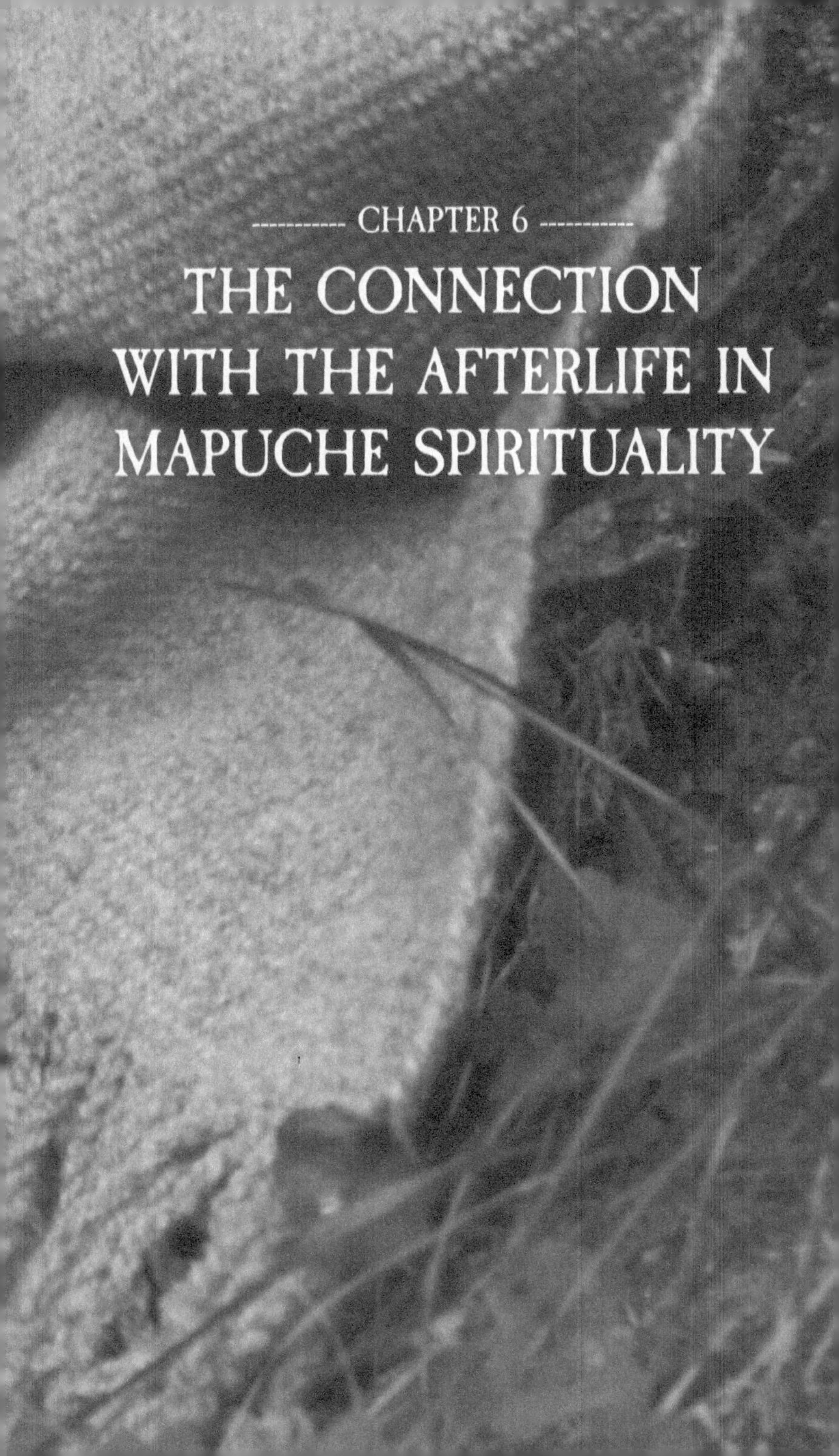

The conception of death and the afterlife

The Mapuche worldview includes a comprehensive vision of life and death. Both realities are interdependent parts of an endless cycle that connects human beings with the environment and their ancestors. Death is not an abrupt end, but rather a transition to a different existence, which remains linked to descendants and the physical world. Thus, life unfolds as a constant interaction between the visible and invisible dimensions. Ancestors and the forces of nature maintain the balance that sustains the harmony of the community.

Within this framework, death is understood as a passage to a new stage, the displacement of a being to a higher realm. This *trawün*, or "encounter," takes place at the end of earthly existence, when the spirit of the deceased begins its journey toward the *Wenu Mapu*, the "land above." This is not a physical space but an ethereal dimension, inhabited by elemental forces such as the sun, the moon, and the ancestors, who guide and accompany the newcomer. The *machi* guides the spirit to overcome obstacles and achieve lasting peace in this sacred space.

The process of transition to the *Wenu Mapu* does not happen suddenly. It involves a series of stages that must be carefully respected. The community participates in ceremonies that allow the spirit of the deceased to move toward its destination without interruption or stumbling. In these rites, the *machis* act as mediators between the earthly world and the afterlife. They ensure that the spirit does not become a soul trapped on the earthly plane. According to Mapuche beliefs, when the journey to *Wenu Mapu* is not completed properly, the spirit remains in *Nag mapu*, or "earthly world," creating disorder that affects both the community and the elements of nature. Restless entities manifest their existence in disturbing ways, often through natural phenomena or by creating discomfort among the living. To counteract this possibility, the community gathers in ceremonies that include prayers, offerings, and songs intended to facilitate the spirit's journey to *Wenu Mapu*. These celebrations ensure that the soul departs in peace, with the support of its loved ones, and joins the ancestors without negatively affecting the environment or daily life. Unlike the Western conception, death is not perceived as an end, but as a transition to a form of presence that allows the deceased to continue to intervene in the destiny of the community.

Ancestors as spiritual guides

Ancestors occupy a central place for the Mapuche people: they are active and constant forces that guide, protect, and enrich community life. Honoring them is a responsibility that involves preserving their teachings and values. They act as guides and protectors of the community, observing from a different dimension and actively participating in the events of daily life, especially in the face of uncertainty or conflict. They are not conceived as passive or aloof figures, but as guardians of the living, capable of intervening in the lives of their descendants.

The influence of ancestors is evident in decisions regarding the distribution of resources, the organization of events, and the resolution of disputes. Their teachings guide the decisions of the leaders and serve as a basis for deliberation, ensuring that well-being and social cohesion remain intact.

The ancestors' protection is also evident in the face of external adversities, such as confrontations with other communities or extreme weather events. In such situations, the community turns to them for intervention and protection. In the event of droughts or floods, the Mapuche perform ceremonies to protect the community. The belief in the protective power of ancestors reinforces the conviction that they continue to watch over and protect them.

The worlds of the living and the ancestors are not rigidly separated. The spirits of the ancestors reside in places in the environment, such as mountains, rivers, and forests, and weave a symbolic network that enables communication and exchange. Natural phenomena are often interpreted as expressions of the ancestors, who manifest themselves through these elements to guide and warn the community about possible risks or disharmonies.

There are Mapuche stories about ancestors communicating with the living, especially in times of crisis or crucial decisions. The teachings and warnings of the ancestors serve as moral guidelines for the daily life of the community. The intervention of the *machi* and the rituals of consulting the ancestors underscore a fundamental interdependence between the living and the dead, where both contribute to collective well-being and balance.

Sacred altars, *rewes*, are access points for meeting with ancestors. They are located in natural spaces of symbolic importance, such as ancient trees or high peaks, which facilitate the connection with the transcendent. During rituals such as the *ngillatun*, the Mapuche people express gratitude, respect, and devotion to their ancestors; they ask for their protection and advice to ensure the peace and well-being of the group. These ceremonies allow for symbolic interaction between the living and the dead, in a space of reciprocity where the ancestors act as protectors and guides.

The legacy of the ancestors is kept alive through oral narratives and rituals that strengthen family and social cohesion. For the Mapuche, the departure of an individual does not imply the loss of his or her teachings; on the contrary, the knowledge of the ancestors is preserved and transmitted through *epew*, traditional stories that communicate the history and values of the community. These stories consolidate collective identity and allow current generations to act in accordance with ancestral principles, ensuring cultural continuity that guides everyday actions.

In the ceremonial dance *purrun*, the Mapuche people pay homage to their ancestors. This dance is a manifestation of cultural renewal. Each movement and each song celebrates belonging, consolidates lineage, and ensures that the ancestral legacy remains alive and retains its meaning in all areas of community life.

Pewma: dreams as means of spiritual communication

In Mapuche culture, the dream state is a central means of communication with higher forces and ancestral entities. This perception of dreams is not limited to individual experience, but is a mechanism deeply integrated into the social and cultural dynamics of the Mapuche people, connecting the dreamer to a network of meanings and links to the invisible world. The dream, or *pewma*, is a form of revelation, an opening that brings knowledge and warnings that can only be understood with the help of the *machi*, who interprets these messages.

Dreams are not considered private fantasies or projections of the subconscious, as modern psychology suggests. On the contrary, in the dream state, the dreamer's soul comes into contact with a transcendent plane, where truths or teachings are revealed that can have repercussions on personal life and the community. Dreams are prophetic: they guide, point the way, anticipate events, and warn of imminent dangers.

From this perspective, dreams are not ordinary events or passive experiences, but moments of openness to realities that transcend everyday understanding.

The *machi*'s wisdom and ability to interpret dreams is an essential attribute that confers legitimacy and authority in the community. Dream interpretation is a complex task that requires knowledge accumulated over generations, as well as a keen understanding of the symbols and messages that appear in the world of dreams. This work is neither arbitrary nor capricious, but is based on a rigorous system of meanings, in which each element of the dream has a specific value within a broader context.

Interpreting the *pewma* is a meticulous practice that involves observing the details of the dream and the dreamer. *Machis* seek to unravel the message hidden behind the images, scenes, or dream entities and determine their relevance to the individual and the community. *Pewma* manifests spiritual connections that reflect the state of the dreamer and the overall balance between the natural and supernatural forces surrounding the community.

Each dream is examined in light of that balance. The interpretation seeks to restore or preserve harmony between the visible and invisible worlds. Dream interpretation involves a careful reading of symbols that appear in the *pewma*. Animals, natural elements, and colors carry specific meanings. Animals can symbolize forces or spirits with which the dreamer has a particular connection. A bird, a fox, or a puma can be interpreted in different ways depending on the context and the dreamer's relationship with their environment. The appearance of water, fire, or trees can have different meanings, which the *machi* evaluates according to the person's situation.

Dreams reveal information about the future and reflect the dreamer's spiritual and emotional health. *Machis* can identify possible imbalances or internal conflicts that could affect the individual and the community. The *pewma* is a spiritual diagnosis that allows the *machi* to intervene through rituals, offerings, and prayers to restore harmony and avoid negative consequences.

Dreams can also contain community messages, such as calls to perform specific ceremonies or warnings about possible misfortunes. Dreams that reveal imbalances in the community can motivate the performance of collective rituals to prevent conflict or ensure peace. In these ceremonies, community members express their respect and devotion to the entities that manifest themselves through the *pewma*, understanding that such messages are signs of the ongoing connection between the community and the invisible world.

The *machi*'s position as a dream interpreter carries an ethical and moral sensitivity that allows her to guide the community in times of crisis. She must contextualize dreams within a framework of traditional values and norms. This work of mediation between the visible and invisible worlds requires empathy and a keen understanding of social dynamics.

Dream interpretation requires intensive learning. From an early age, those with a special gift for understanding the dream world are identified by their elders and receive special training. This learning encompasses symbols and rituals, as well as a sensitivity to the needs and concerns of the community. The oral transmission of this knowledge ensures the continuity of ancestral wisdom and guarantees that the *pewma* remains a source of guidance and support.

Within this training process, direct contact with nature is essential, as natural elements play a fundamental role in dream interpretation. The *machi* learns to relate dream symbols to natural phenomena and to give them a broader meaning, linked to the reality experienced by the community. *Pewma* are not interpreted in isolation, but in the light of a broader ecological, social, and cultural context.

It is important to note that the interpretation of *pewma* is not standardized; *machis* develop their own method and style. The diversity of interpretations reflects the richness of the Mapuche worldview, in which the dream world is perceived as a dynamic and multifaceted space, open to multiple readings and meanings. *Machis* use their own perspective and sensitivity to adapt interpretations to the needs of each person and situation, thus preserving the flexibility and adaptability of the tradition.

In addition to being a means of communication, dreams are a tool for self-knowledge. The Mapuche can explore aspects of their identity and personal history that would otherwise remain hidden or repressed. Dream interpretation allows access to a deep dimension of the mind and spirit. It touches on fears, desires, and memories that are important for personal growth and transformation.

Pewma helps connect with ancestors, who offer guidance and protection. Dreams about ancestors are special, since they are interpreted as direct messages from those souls who have reached *Wenu Mapu* and watch over the welfare of the community. This is a reminder of the continuous presence of the dead among the living. It is also an opportunity for dreamers to receive teachings that strengthen traditions and family lineages. Contact with ancestors implies that death is not a definitive break. The intervention of the ancestors in the *pewma* confirms the belief in an unbreakable connection between the visible and invisible worlds, where the dead become protectors and guides for those who remain on the earthly plane.

Dreams and their interpretations are an integral component of the Mapuche social and cultural structure. They enable communication with higher forces that help maintain community cohesion. Each dream is a bridge to dimensions beyond immediate reality, and a source of wisdom that nourishes and orients the community.

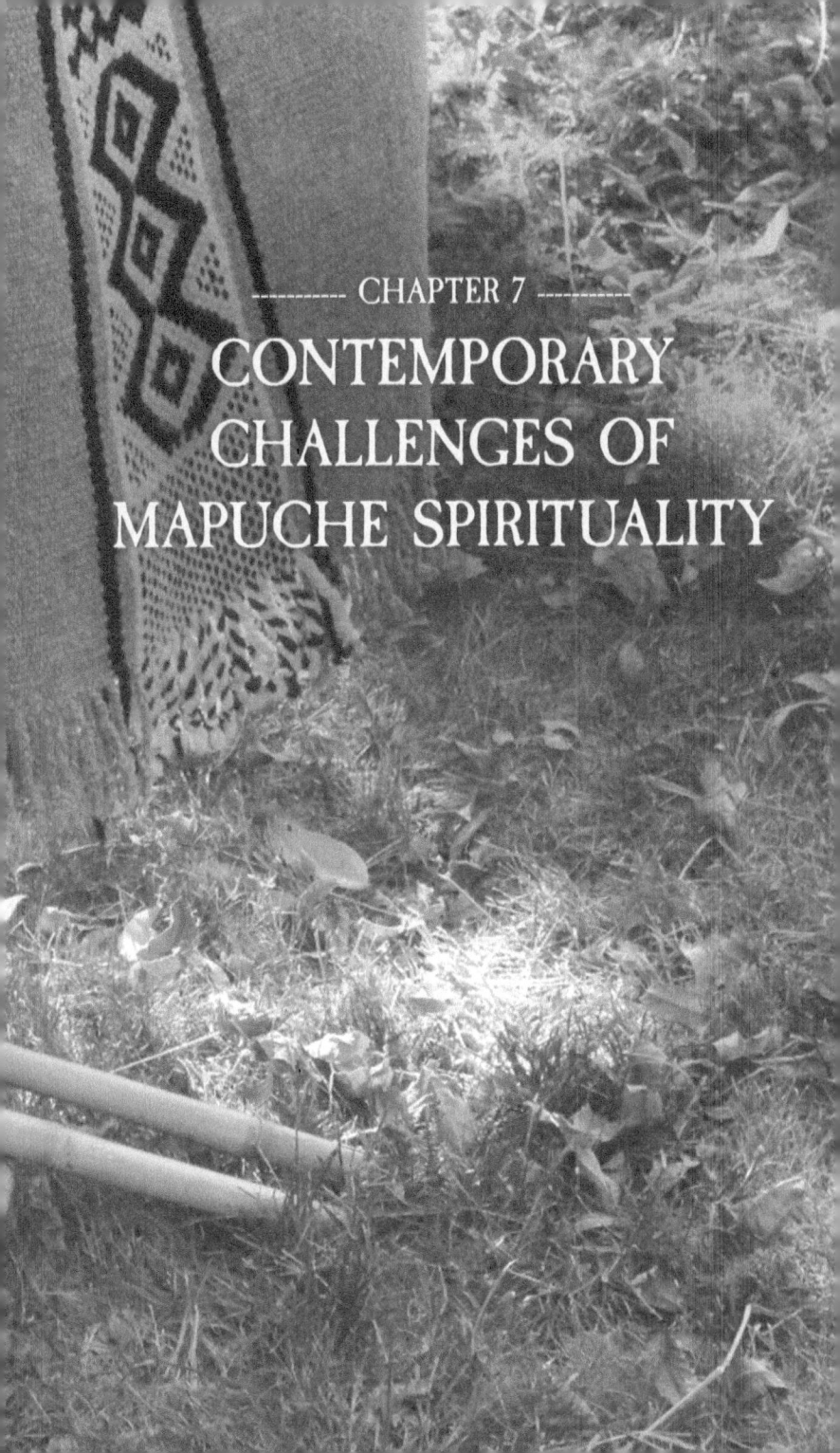

CHAPTER 7

CONTEMPORARY CHALLENGES OF MAPUCHE SPIRITUALITY

The impact of modernity and urbanization on spiritual practices

Today, Mapuche culture faces the challenges of rapid modernization and urbanization, which have transformed the environments where ceremonies were traditionally held. Modernity has physically altered spaces, forced new lifestyles, and significantly affected customs transmitted through generations.

The Mapuche worldview, therefore, faces the need to reaffirm and redefine itself in order to persist in a rapidly changing environment.

Historically, Mapuche life took place in non-urban spaces with forests, mountains, and rivers. These physical places are also spaces of transcendence charged with deep symbolism. Each place has a particular meaning that facilitates contact and cultural protection. However, the advance of cities has restricted access to such places, limiting the possibility of performing ceremonies in their entirety, as many depend on direct interaction with the natural world. In urban areas, the traditional link with the territory faces tangible difficulties: people must adapt their ceremonies to enclosed or improvised spaces and overcome obstacles that complicate respect for specific places identified for their relevance and where the *ngen* dwell.

Urban expansion also changes the rhythm of Mapuche life. In cities, days tend to be rigorous, leaving little time for introspection and ceremonial preparation. As a

Chapter 7: Contemporary challenges of Mapuche spirituality

result, some rituals have been abbreviated or shortened, with a consequent reduction in their symbolic richness and cultural depth.

Urban life also hinders the oral transmission of knowledge. In traditional settings, elders occupy a central place in the cultural legacy. However, in cities, people live apart, disrupting oral transmissions. Young people do not maintain constant and meaningful interactions with their elders. This leads to a loss of access to cultural knowledge, as well as a reinterpretation of symbols in contexts far removed from their original references.

Faced with these obstacles, various urban Mapuche groups have found alternative ways to preserve their culture. Many gather in community centers which, although they do not substitute for natural sacred spaces, allow them to perform ceremonies that preserve cultural identity. These places also serve to educate young people about their heritage and enable them to participate in activities guided by community leaders and elders.

A clear example is the *ngillatun* ceremony. Traditionally, it requires a *rewe*, but in urban contexts, portable or symbolic altars are used. This allows the same ceremony to be performed. Since the substitute *rewe* and the urban environment do not carry the intrinsic symbolism of nature in its traditional places, part of the essence and original meaning of the rite is lost.

The urban education system is a significant obstacle to cultural preservation. In cities, educational institutions emphasize Western values, leaving little room for indigenous teachings. Mapuche children and young people who attend these schools are educated in a system that ignores and undervalues their cultural heritage. This exclusion reinforces processes of assimilation and, in certain cases, the internalization of prejudices that distort their identity. Ties to their roots are weakened and a disconnect from traditions occurs, with the risk of misinterpreting their own heritage.

To address these challenges, some communities have promoted alternative educational programs aimed at strengthening cultural identity and ancestral knowledge. These programs include teaching Mapudungun, Mapuche history, and ceremonies, with the aim of creating an environment where young people can reconcile their identity with urban life. However, such initiatives face barriers to integration into the formal system, as they depend on the collaboration of institutions that recognize the importance of cultural diversity. Even so, they are fundamental efforts to revitalize identity in a context where modernity tends to displace traditional customs and values.

Working life presents significant challenges for those who live in the city. Urban jobs demand considerable time and effort, often with inflexible schedules, making it difficult to participate in ceremonies and community activities. This tension has prompted adjustments to ritual calendars to accommodate urban life. It is especially difficult to prepare for ceremonies that require everyone's participation.

Likewise, the urban economic logic, oriented toward consumption and competitiveness, conflicts with a culture based on cooperation and respect for ways of life. Traditional Mapuche values prioritize balance and interdependence with nature. Those who seek to live according to these principles face individualism and material accumulation.

In response, some Mapuche individuals and communities have adopted alternative economic approaches, such as urban agriculture and fair trade. These activities are consistent with their heritage and allow them to integrate principles of respect for the environment and sustainability. Such projects provide livelihoods while preserving Mapuche values.

Politically, communities in Chile and Argentina face structural barriers and discrimination that limit the free expression of their cultural identity. This marginalization causes a disconnect from traditions and a perception that their culture is not valued or constitutes an obstacle to urban integration. The lack of spaces to freely practice their cultural customs has prompted constant mobilization in favor of cultural diversity in cities.

Through urban collectives, the Mapuche people have worked to achieve recognition, demanding adequate spaces for their ceremonies from local authorities. Through demonstrations, cultural events, and alliances with human rights organizations, they have sought to raise awareness about the relevance of their traditions and the urgency of protecting their rights in urban environments.

Globalization and international trends also have an impact on cultural preservation. Exposure to outside ideas has led to the integration of elements from other traditions into certain ceremonies, creating syncretism that, while enriching, risks diluting cultural essence. This phenomenon poses a significant challenge for those who seek to remain faithful to authentic practices.

Despite this, the Mapuche people have shown remarkable resilience and adaptability. The constant search for methods to preserve their customs, the creation of spaces for identity expression, and the reorganization of their ceremonies demonstrate a determined effort to sustain a cultural heritage that continues to be a fundamental component of Mapuche identity today.

Resilience and revitalization of Mapuche spirituality and shamanism

In recent decades, the Mapuche people, who are mainly settled in southern Chile and Argentina, have embarked on a struggle to preserve and revitalize their culture and traditions. This resistance is a response to a prolonged process of colonization and territorial uprooting. The struggle is taking place in a global context of cultural homogenization and economic modernization that threatens to erase indigenous traditions in the name of progress. For the Mapuche, the path to cultural revitalization is not a simple exercise in remembering ceremonies and rituals; it is a deliberate effort to reestablish their identity and collective values, which express a worldview radically different from Western visions of reality.

Language is a means of cultural resistance. Mapudungun is a tool for everyday communication and the main vehicle for transmitting their knowledge and values. Each term contains a network of symbolic meanings that establishes intrinsic links between individuals and the environment. Revitalizing Mapudungun means preserving an interpretation of the world in which nature and the cosmos occupy a central place and transcend mundane conceptions.

Integration policies have pushed the Mapuche people into a process of forced assimilation that threatens to make their culture disappear for the sake of a dominant identity. This trend has been resisted through the reaffirmation of traditional values and knowledge, in an attempt to preserve a cultural identity that challenges hegemonic norms. Mapuche resistance manifests itself as an active recovery of ceremonies and rituals, acts that reaffirm the link with the territory, the ancestors, and the forces that govern nature. These rituals might be misinterpreted as simple cultural practices, but they actually constitute a complex system of meanings that allows the Mapuche to keep their way of life and fundamental principles alive.

A central component of this cultural resistance is the recovery of natural spaces considered sacred. These are fundamental places for ceremonies. They are points of convergence between cosmic forces and everyday reality, charged with energy that must be respected and cared for. Urban growth and industrial development threaten their access to these places. In response, resistance movements have taken steps to reclaim these spaces, demanding the right to perform their ceremonies there without interference. For the Mapuche, the integrity of sacred sites is essential, since the authenticity of their ceremonies depends on a genuine connection with the land and the energies that inhabit it. The loss of these territories, and the consequent impossibility of performing ceremonies there, represents a threat to the continuity of their culture and worldview.

The figure of the *machi* symbolizes a form of resistance to modernity, embodying an alternative worldview that challenges Western notions of health and balance. Training a *machi* is a long apprenticeship that includes complex ceremonial practices. However, social changes and the fragmentation of community life have made this training process difficult, as many young Mapuche have migrated to urban areas, where the connection with traditional culture is weakening. Despite these challenges, communities have promoted initiatives to train new *machis*, thus ensuring the continuity of this ancestral knowledge.

The preservation of instruments such as the *kultrun* and the *trutruka* is a priority in cultural revitalization

Chapter 7: Contemporary challenges of Mapuche spirituality

movements, as they are essential for rituals and symbolize the continuity of the Mapuche cosmovision.

Oral tradition, composed of stories and myths, plays a central role in the transmission of values and beliefs. These stories explain the origins of nature and ethical norms. Myths and legends describe the exploits and teachings of ancestors; they communicate respect for nature and the importance of living in harmony with all beings. Through these stories, the Mapuche preserve their history and value system, which allows them to understand their place in the world. Revitalization movements promote the preservation of this oral tradition by organizing gatherings where elders share their knowledge with younger people.

In recent decades, cultural revitalization movements have celebrated ceremonies such as the *ngillatun* and the *We tripantu* in urban contexts, adapting them to new realities without losing their essence. Thus, the Mapuche community keeps its identity alive even in environments that are often hostile or alien to its customs.

Faced with a world that pushes for cultural assimilation, the Mapuche people have reaffirmed their identity through traditional practices. Their ceremonies, language, and knowledge have become tools of resistance and vindication of their ancestral rights, consolidating their identity in a global context that often ignores them. Cultural revitalization is a constant affirmation of their worldview and their right to exist as an autonomous and diverse people in a world that threatens their cultural continuity.

Intercultural dialogue and global spirituality

Ancient Mapuche wisdom constitutes a framework of values that offers a way of understanding the universe and existence as a whole. The interdependence of beings and the environment is fundamental. This knowledge is not a set of isolated rituals or beliefs, but an integral philosophy that encompasses all dimensions of life: natural, social, and cultural. In the context of global diversity, this vision is particularly relevant, as it highlights the possibility of conceiving of human beings not as entities separate from the natural world, but as parts of a greater balance, in which each element has a defined role and responsibility toward others.

Intercultural contact with the Mapuche worldview requires openness to other modes of knowledge, without imposing the categories and structures of Western philosophy. To understand Mapuche knowledge in all its depth, it is essential to recognize its specificity and holistic nature, which integrates material and symbolic aspects into a single whole. Mapuche wisdom should not be reduced to decontextualized fragments or interpreted through foreign paradigms. It must be approached with a willingness to learn and listen, allowing this knowledge to reveal its own internal logic and coherence.

Given the contemporary difficulty of oral transmission, intercultural education can be a strategic tool for preserving Mapuche knowledge and ensuring its continuity. Including this knowledge in educational systems would allow for the revaluation of their culture and the integration of their knowledge into the education of new generations. This approach should not be limited to superficial incorporation but should be granted the same legitimacy as Western sciences. This would help to protect Mapuche knowledge and build a society that is more respectful of diversity and aware of the need to safeguard the natural balance.

Legislation is another means of preserving Mapuche traditions. In many cases, the territorial rights of indigenous communities have been violated and natural resource exploitation projects have been implemented without respect for the sacred and vital spaces of these communities. Convention 169 of the International Labor Organization (ILO) represents an important step in the defense of indigenous rights, requiring consultation with indigenous communities before making decisions that may affect their territories or ways of life. However, for these provisions to be implemented, a real commitment is required on the part of national governments, which must recognize the importance of this knowledge and the need to protect a cultural heritage that enriches the world's diversity.

Digital technology offers new possibilities for preserving Mapuche knowledge, but it also poses challenges. Digitization can help document and transmit knowledge and make it available to future generations. However, taken out of context, there is a risk that this knowledge will be misinterpreted, decontextualized, or even commercialized. To avoid this, it is essential that Mapuche communities retain control of their own archives and digital resources and define clear terms for their use and dissemination.

Another way to enrich and strengthen Mapuche knowledge lies in exchange with other philosophical and cultural traditions. This intercultural dialogue should not become the imposition of one set of values on another, but rather a space for mutual learning, in which each tradition contributes its principles and visions to address shared challenges. The Mapuche worldview can offer alternatives in terms of environmental sustainability, while other cultures can contribute complementary approaches to issues of social organization or ethics. This type of interaction allows for the construction of a network of knowledge and values that enriches and strengthens cultural identities in a globalized context.

Mapuche knowledge offers universal lessons applicable to contemporary issues affecting all of humanity. The climate crisis, the loss of biodiversity, and social fragmentation are global challenges that require new ways of thinking and acting. The Mapuche worldview, with its emphasis on balance and interdependence, can provide an ethical and philosophical basis for addressing these issues from a perspective that prioritizes the well-being of the whole over individual interests. This holistic approach, centered on a harmonious relationship with the environment, can inspire significant transformations in the way humanity relates to nature and other cultures.

Chapter 7: Contemporary challenges of Mapuche spirituality

The process of protecting and revitalizing Mapuche knowledge requires special sensitivity and deep respect for their values and beliefs. In an increasingly interconnected world, it is essential that cultures be able to learn from each other without any of them losing their essence or being forced to renounce their identity. Contact with other traditions can enrich identities, but it also risks losing authenticity in an attempt to adapt to a globalized environment. The survival of this ancestral knowledge could be a source of learning and reflection for other cultures, which could be inspired to develop a more respectful and balanced relationship with nature and with other human beings.

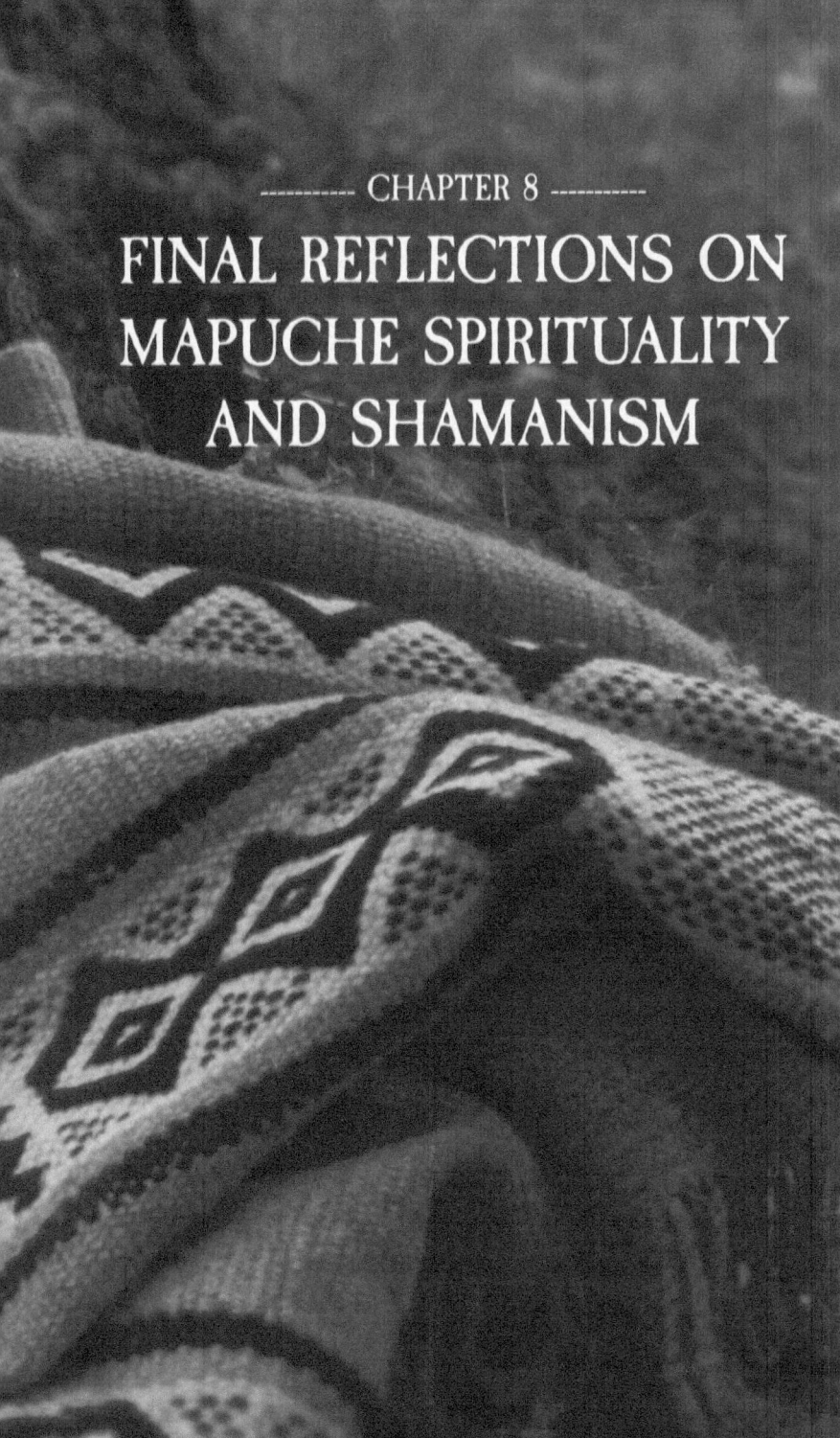

CHAPTER 8
FINAL REFLECTIONS ON MAPUCHE SPIRITUALITY AND SHAMANISM

The Mapuche cosmovision as an alternative for a world in crisis

The Mapuche worldview unfolds like a symbolic fabric that interweaves human existence and nature. For this people, human beings are not isolated, but nodes in a vast network of interdependent relationships that encompass the visible and the invisible. This is not a set of abstract beliefs; it is a philosophy of life in which every human act must be governed by principles of respect, reciprocity, and balance, especially in relation to non-human beings. In a global context marked by unprecedented environmental crises and a marked disconnect between humanity and nature, the Mapuche paradigm of integration and coexistence with the natural world offers valuable lessons for rethinking the prevailing economic trend of extraction and consumption.

A central concept in the Mapuche worldview is *itrofillmogen*, which can be translated as "the totality of life forms." This term covers biodiversity, but also an interdependent totality that recognizes that all beings, regardless of their size or function, possess intrinsic dignity and play an indispensable role in the balance of existence. Nature is a sacred and symbiotic space where life is sustained. While the Western worldview often reduces nature to resources to be extracted, *itrofillmogen* contemplates a living universe. The relational structure formed by *itrofillmogen* and the *ngen* is more than a description of the natural world: above all, it constitutes a system of ethical values and a way of existence in which human beings interact constantly with their environment. They are its caretakers, not its owners. Responsibility is pressing, as each act affects the entire network and therefore requires ethical reflection on immediate interests and collective harmony. In this web of relationships, humans are no longer at the center but become just another element in a flow of life that demands reciprocity and respect.

A person's well-being can only be understood within the framework of their community and their relationship with nature. Every individual healing process has a collective and, ultimately, ecological dimension. This holistic conception of health and balance is inseparable from the Mapuche concept of sustainability. In the Mapuche worldview, sustainability is not a secondary objective or a temporary response to the recent environmental crisis, but an essential principle that permeates all areas of life. Taking responsibility for maintaining the natural balance is a duty imposed on each generation, as all human intervention must be carried out with a vision for the future and deep respect for the needs of the environment.

The notion of community is also central to the Mapuche worldview. It is a principle of social organization that transcends human relationships. The community is a collective organism in which each individual contributes to the general welfare and preserving equilibrium. This vision differs radically from the individualism that characterizes many modern societies, where personal interest often prevails over the common good.

This perception of community also includes a temporal and ethical dimension, as present actions inevitably have an impact on future generations. Respect for those who are not yet born is a fundamental premise; the community includes its past, present, and future members. Responsibility toward the future stands as an alternative ethical model to the more common short-term approach. The Mapuche vision encourages an ethical evaluation of each act, considering both its immediate implications and its lasting effects on the environment and the social fabric. By promoting an ethic of respect and sustainability, this worldview offers a valuable alternative to current models of development and consumption.

The community structure of Mapuche society also represents an alternative model of social organization in an era marked by fragmentation and individualism. The Mapuche conception of community, based on cooperation and respect for future generations, offers a way to address the crises of meaning and difficulties afflicting contemporary societies. This value system does not seek to idealize a mythical past, but rather suggests a possibility of living in the present in a way that is more in tune with nature and in communion with future generations. In a world in crisis, this perspective offers an alternative for reconnecting humanity with the planet and with the beings that inhabit it, proposing a relationship based on care and ethical commitment to life in all its forms.

Connections between Mapuche spirituality and other indigenous traditions

The *nguillatun* ritual recognizes human interdependence with the environment. It is performed collectively and reflects a strong sense of community, emphasizing the idea that the well-being of each member depends on the harmony of all. Other indigenous cultures, such as the Hopi and Zuñi, hold similar ceremonies to ask the natural forces for fertility and abundant harvests. In contrast, the *nguillatun* emphasizes the shared responsibility of sustaining reciprocity with the environment.

The role of ancestors in Mapuche culture can be compared to veneration practices in Mesoamerica, where ancestral figures are also conceived as protectors of their descendants. However, for the Mapuche, the link is direct and not limited to annual festivities; it responds to the needs of the moment and the natural cycles of the community.

The Mapuche set of norms known as *admapu* can be compared to the *Kichwa* concept of *kawsak sacha* (Living Forest) of the indigenous peoples of the Andes and the Ecuadorian Amazon, which demands respect and ethical connections with the forest. However, *admapu* also incorporates specific community elements that give it a unique depth.

While in some indigenous cultures of the Amazon the vitality of animals and plants is invoked or channeled in specific rituals, the Mapuche worldview advocates a relationship of deep respect and restraint, aimed at preserving life in all its forms and ensuring that any intervention in the environment is ethical and justified.

The Mapuche conception of health is understood as a state of balance that transcends the physical and includes harmony between individuals, communities, and nature. *Machis* are once again key figures, as they can restore harmony through rituals that heal the person and reconcile their relationship with the forces that govern the universe. This community-based approach to healing resembles that of the Lakota, where an individual's imbalance can affect the community as a whole and the healer acts as an intermediary between invisible forces and the physical world. In the Mapuche tradition, this healing process is closely linked to the cycles and rhythms of the earth, adding a distinctive ecological dimension that rarely appears in other indigenous worldviews.

Over the centuries, the Mapuche have shown a remarkable ability to adapt to cultural transformations, integrating elements from other belief systems without losing the coherence of their own worldview. This process of assimilation has not involved renouncing their original values and has strengthened their ability to reinterpret external influences. It can be compared to what happened among the Maya or the Quechua, who also incorporated elements of Western religions during the colonial period, but not through thoughtless syncretism. In the Mapuche case, cultural reinterpretation is carried out with caution: each new element is evaluated according to its compatibility with the principles of the Mapuche worldview, thus preserving the authenticity and autonomy of their ancestral culture.

The Mapuche spiritual heritage and its legacy for future generations

The cultural heritage of the Mapuche people is a complex network of meanings and knowledge that reflect a way of understanding the world deeply rooted in the harmonious relationship between human beings and the natural universe. This heritage, present in southern Chile and Argentina, is built on a series of fundamental principles that have survived numerous attempts at assimilation and displacement, remaining valid throughout the centuries. Mapuche culture is manifested in ceremonies and extends to a conception of the world that connects all dimensions of life, promoting an integrative and holistic vision of being.

Globalization has jeopardized the continuity of this ancestral vision. The transmission of Mapuche knowledge and identity faces a constant challenge, especially among the younger generations who, in many cases, have grown up disconnected from their cultural roots and the Mapudungun language. The progressive loss of this language constitutes an obstacle to communication and hinders the transmission of ideas and knowledge deeply rooted in Mapuche thought, as the language encapsulates meanings and values that have no equivalent in other languages. Therefore, the preservation of Mapudungun is not simply a linguistic issue, but an effort to safeguard access to a broader and more diverse knowledge that defines the cultural identity of the people.

In Mapuche communities, the wise men or guides, or *ngenpin*, play an essential role in preserving and teaching these values. They conduct ceremonies and act as custodians of the history, oral tradition, and stories that structure Mapuche identity. They convey to young people the importance of ties to the land and to their ancestors, teaching them to interpret the environment from a perspective that transcends the visible. In their stories, the *mapu* is a sacred space that connects the past and the present, placing each individual in a network of relationships that includes both the living and the ancestors. The knowledge they transmit is, therefore, a fundamental means of strengthening Mapuche identity and forging an authentic connection with the environment and history.

However, formal education in Chile and Argentina has historically shown a notable omission of Mapuche knowledge, which has contributed to a progressive disconnection between young people and their roots. In response, a cultural and educational movement has emerged in recent decades that seeks to recover and raise the profile of this knowledge within the school system. This momentum has materialized in bilingual intercultural education programs, designed so that Mapuche children and young people can learn in their mother tongue and acquire a deeper understanding of their values and customs. The incorporation of Mapudungun in the classroom is a fundamental step toward reestablishing the link between the younger generations and their cultural heritage and strengthening their sense of community belonging.

Intercultural education, in addition to facilitating language learning, promotes respect and appreciation for nature and the Mapuche social structure. These programs integrate content that includes stories and beliefs about the *ngen* and the *pillans*. Children learn about their culture, developing pride and respect for their identity in the process. These values are essential in an era characterized by cultural homogenization, as they allow young people to keep their heritage alive through diversity and pluralism.

At the same time, many communities have taken the initiative to offer community education and learning opportunities where young people can acquire traditional techniques in pottery, weaving, and medicine. These crafts serve as vehicles for transmitting knowledge deeply rooted in interaction with the environment. Pottery and weaving, for example, are not mere decorative or utilitarian objects, but creations loaded with symbolism and ancestral knowledge. By learning these traditions, young people acquire a broader understanding of balance with nature, as each material and form has its own meaning within the Mapuche cultural structure.

Traditional Mapuche medicine is based on a detailed and respectful understanding of the properties of plants and other natural elements. A set of health practices that are part of a holistic system integrating body, mind, and environment are passed down from generation to generation. Those who learn these practices acquire concrete skills while developing a deep respect for natural resources and the wisdom of their ancestors. This approach, distinct from Western medical treatment, offers an alternative understanding of health and well-being by recognizing the role of invisible forces in healing and connecting with the environment.

In a global context where environmental crisis and ecosystem degradation have become critical issues, the cultural legacy of the Mapuche people offers an invaluable perspective for rethinking the relationship between humans and nature. The Mapuche worldview, with its emphasis on reciprocity and the interdependence of all forms of life, presents an ethical and ecological alternative that invites reflection. For Mapuche thought, the environment is not a resource to be exploited, but a set of entities with which humans must maintain a balanced and mutually respectful relationship. This vision can inspire contemporary approaches to sustainability and conservation, underscoring the need for an environmental ethic that values balance and coexistence.

This cultural legacy, far from being limited to the Mapuche identity, has the potential to enrich the practices and values of other societies, offering a model of coexistence and respect for biological and cultural diversity. Similarly, the preservation of Mapuche culture represents an opportunity to revalue ancestral knowledge as part of humanity's cultural heritage, especially in the face of current environmental and social challenges. Future generations can find in the Mapuche worldview an ethical guide for addressing contemporary problems, recognizing that every being has a role and value in the fabric of life. This cultural heritage and its transmission can serve as a guideline for building a society that values cultural and natural diversity, integrating this knowledge into educational, social, and environmental spheres.

The Mapuche cultural legacy can therefore be conceived as a repository of knowledge and ethical principles applicable to the conservation and respect of nature. This worldview invites reflection on the need to cultivate an awareness that recognizes the value of all forms of life and encourages a balanced and responsible relationship between human beings and their environment.

Appendices

Prabhuji
H.H. Avadhūta Bhaktivedānta Yogācārya
Śrī Ramakrishnananda Bābājī Mahārāja

About Prabhuji

Prabhuji is a realized master, a universalist Advaita mystic, and an authorized representative of Hinduism. His profound religious dedication is expressed through his artistic work as a writer and painter. In recognition of his spiritual attainment, his guru has conferred upon him the title of *avadhūta*. He has developed the Retroprogressive Path, an original contribution rooted in the inclusive principles of *Sanātana Dharma*, an ancient tradition to which he maintains a formal and constant adherence.

His solid background includes a doctorate in *Vaiṣṇava* philosophy, awarded by the prestigious Jiva Institute of Vedic Studies in Vrindavan, India, and a doctorate in Yogic philosophy earned at Yoga-Samskrutham University. These doctorates reaffirm his commitment to traditional teachings and his connection to the spiritual roots of the Hindu religion.

Prabhuji has dedicated more than fifty years to the exploration and practice of different religions, philosophies, paths of liberation, and spiritual disciplines. He has absorbed the teachings of great masters, shamans, priests, machis, shifus, roshis, shaykhs, daoshis, yogis, pastors, swamis, rabbis, kabbalists, monks, gurus, philosophers, sages, and saints whom he personally visited during his years of searching. He has lived in many places and traveled the world, thirsting for Truth.

In 2011, with the blessings of his Gurudeva, Prabhuji adopted the path of a secluded *bhajanānandī* and withdrew from society to lead the contemplative life of a hermit. Since then, he has been living as an independent Messianic-Marian Hindu religious hermit. His days have been spent in solitude, praying, writing, painting, and meditating in silence and contemplation. His *iṣṭa-devatā*, or "chosen deity," is Lord Yeshua, understood from the traditional Hindu perspective as the *avatāra*, the "incarnate God" in whom he centers his devotion. Unlike the interpretation of Western Christianity, his connection with Yeshua arises from the Semitic roots of the historical Jesus, within the original Hebrew horizon of his revelation.

Prabhuji is the sole disciple of H.D.G. Avadhūta Śrī Brahmānanda Bābājī Mahārāja, who in turn is one of the closest and most intimate disciples of H.D.G. Avadhūta Śrī Mastarāma Bābājī Mahārāja.

Prabhuji was appointed as the successor of the lineage by his master, who conferred upon him the responsibility of continuing the sacred *paramparā* of *avadhūtas*, officially appointing him as guru and ordering him to serve as Ācārya successor under the name H.H. Avadhūta Bhaktivedānta Yogācārya Śrī Ramakrishnananda Bābājī Mahārāja.

Prabhuji is also a disciple of H.D.G. Bhakti-kavi Atulānanda Ācārya Mahārāja, who is a direct disciple of H.D.G. A.C. Bhaktivedānta Swami Prabhupāda. We could say that Gurudeva Atulānanda affectionately assumed the role of guide during his initial stage of learning, and because he was Prabhuji's first guru, he is considered a fundamental part of his evolutionary process. For his part, Guru Mahārāja was Prabhuji's second and last guru and provided him with guidance during his advanced stage. Gurudeva acted as the primary educator at the dawn of his spiritual path, while Guru Mahārāja exercised with great diligence the role of master at the highest level, accompanying him until his realization.

Prabhuji's Hinduism is broad, universal, and pluralistic. Living up to his title of *avadhūta*, his lively and fresh teachings are not confined by any philosophy or religion, even his own. His teachings promote critical thinking and invite us to question our own convictions. The essence of his syncretic vision, the Retroprogressive Path, is self-awareness and the recognition of consciousness. For him, awakening at the level of consciousness, or the transcendence of the egoic phenomenon, is the next step in humanity's evolution.

Prabhuji was born on March 21, 1958, in Santiago, the capital of the Republic of Chile. When he was eight years old, he had a mystical experience that motivated his search for the Truth, or the Ultimate Reality. This transformed his life into an authentic inner and outer pilgrimage. He has completely devoted his life to deepening the early transformative experience that marked the beginning of his process of retroevolution.

From an early age, his father, Yosef Har-Zion ZT"L, and his mother, Frida Lazcano ZT"L, expressed a constant and unconditional love, independent of academic performance or achievements. Prabhuji's paternal grandfather was a distinguished senior officer in the Chilean police, who raised his father Yosef under a strict discipline. Marked by this, Yosef decided to raise his own children in an environment defined by freedom. Prabhuji and his sister were their parents' most cherished endeavors, guided by their trust in life itself as the compass for their choices.

In this context, Prabhuji grew up without experiencing any sense of urgency, demand, or external pressure. From a very young age, he noticed that the educational system prevented him from devoting himself to what truly mattered: learning about himself. At the age of eleven, he decided to stop attending conventional school and devote himself to autodidactic learning. When he chose to leave school in pursuit of his inner quest, his family responded with profound respect and acceptance. Yosef fully supported his son's interests, encouraging him at every step of his search for Truth.

From the age of ten onward, his father shared with him the wisdom of Hebrew spirituality and Western philosophy, fostering an environment of daily discussions that often extended late into the night. In essence, Prabhuji embodied the ideal of freedom and unconditional love that his parents had striven to cultivate within their home.

From a very young age and on his own initiative, Prabhuji began to practice karate and to study Eastern philosophy and religions in a self-taught manner. During his adolescence, no one interfered with his decisions. At the age of 15, he established a deep, intimate, and long friendship with the famous Uruguayan writer and poet Blanca Luz Brum, who was his neighbor on Merced Street in Santiago, Chile. He traveled throughout Chile in search of wise and interesting people from whom he could learn. In southern Chile, he met *machis* who taught him about the rich Mapuche spirituality and shamanism.

In June 1975, at the young age of 17, he earned his first certification as a Yoga Teacher under H.H. Śrī Brahmānanda Sarasvatī (Rāmamurti S. Mishra, M.D.), the founder of the World Yoga University, the Yoga Society of NY, and the Ananda Ashram.

At the age of 18, Prabhuji embraced the monastic discipline through long stays in various ashrams of different Hindu currents (*Gauḍīya* Vaishnavas, Advaita Vedanta, etc.) in Chile and Israel. There, he underwent rigorous training within the Hindu religion. Immersed in the strict observance of religious life, he received a systematic education, following traditional methods of monastic teaching. His training included the in-depth study of sacred scriptures, the practice of austerities, the fulfillment of strict vows, and participation in prescribed rituals, all under the guidance of masters or gurus. Through this intensive discipline, he internalized the fundamental principles of Hindu monastic life, adopting its values, codes of conduct, and contemplative practices. This allowed him to learn the theory and also to incorporate the ideals that characterize the spirituality of Hinduism.

Over the years, Prabhuji became a recognized authority on Eastern wisdom. He is known for his erudition on the *Vaidika* and *Tāntrika* aspects of Hinduism and all branches of yoga (*jñāna, karma, bhakti, haṭha, rāja, kuṇḍalinī, tantra, mantra*, and others). He has an inclusive attitude toward all religions and is intimately familiar with Judaism, Christianity, Buddhism, Islam, Sufism, Taoism, Sikhism, Jainism, Shintoism, Bahaism, Shamanism, and the Mapuche religion, among others.

During his stay in the Middle East, his esteemed friend and scholar, Kamil Shchadi, imparted to him profound knowledge about the Druze faith. He also benefited from his closeness to the revered and wise Salach Abbas, who helped him to reach a thorough understanding of Islam and Sufism. He studied Theravada Buddhism personally from the Venerable W. Medhananda Thero of Sri Lanka. He delved deeper into Christian theology with H.H. Monsignor Iván Larraín Eyzaguirre at the Veracruz Church in Santiago de Chile and with Mr. Héctor Luis Muñoz, who holds a degree in theology from the Universidad Católica de la Santísima Concepción, Chile. His profound studies, his masters' blessings, his research into the sacred scriptures, and his vast teaching experience have earned him international recognition in the field of religion and spirituality.

Prabhuji's curiosity for Western thought led him to venture into the field of philosophy in all its different branches. He specialized in Transcendental Phenomenology and the Phenomenology of Religion. He had the privilege of studying intensively for several years with his uncle Jorge Balazs, philosopher, researcher, and author, who wrote *The world upside-down* under his pen name Gyuri Akos. Prabhuji pursued private studies in mythology and philosophy for four years (1984–1987) under Dr. Meira Laneado of Bar-Ilan University. He studied privately for many years with Dr. Jonathan Ramos, a renowned philosopher, historian, and university professor graduated from the Universidad Católica de Salta, Argentina. He also studied with Dr. Alejandro Cavallazzi Sánchez, who holds an undergraduate degree in philosophy from the Universidad Panamericana, a master's degree in philosophy from the Universidad Iberoamericana, and a doctorate in philosophy from the Universidad Nacional Autónoma de México (UNAM). He also studied privately with Santiago Sánchez Borboa, who holds a PhD in Philosophy from the University of Arizona, USA.

Prabhuji's spiritual quest led him to study with masters from different traditions and to travel far from his native Chile, to places as distant as Israel, Brazil, India, and the United States. He is fluent in Spanish, Hebrew, Portuguese, and English. During his stay in Israel, he furthered his Hebrew and Aramaic studies in order to broaden his knowledge of the sacred scriptures. He studied other languages intensively, such as Sanskrit with Dr. Naga Kanya Kumari Garipathi, from Osmania University in Hyderabad (India); Pali at the Oxford Center for Buddhist Studies; and Latin and Ancient Greek with Professor Ariel Lazcano and later with Javier Alvarez, who holds a degree in Classical Philology from the University of Seville.

Two great masters contributed to Prabhuji's retroprogressive process. In 1976, he met his first guru, H.D.G Bhakti-kavi Atulānanda Ācārya Swami, whom he called Gurudeva. In those days, Gurudeva was a young *brahmacārī* who held the position of president of the ISKCON temple at Eyzaguirre 2404, Puente Alto, Santiago, Chile. Years later, he gave Prabhuji his first initiation, Brahminical initiation, and finally, Prabhuji formally accepted the sacraments of the holy order of *sannyāsa*, becoming a monk of the Brahma Gauḍīya Sampradāya. Gurudeva connected him to the devotion to Kṛṣṇa. He imparted to him the wisdom of bhakti yoga and instructed him in the practice of the *māhā-mantra* and the study of the holy scriptures.

In 1996, Prabhuji met his second guru, H.D.G. Avadhūta Śrī Brahmānanda Bābājī Mahārāja, in Rishikesh, India. Guru Mahārāja, as Prabhuji would call him, revealed that his own master, H.D.G. Avadhūta Śrī Mastarāma Bābājī Mahārāja, had told him years before he died that a person would come from the West and request to be his disciple. He commanded him to accept only that particular seeker. When he asked how he would identify this person, Mastarāma Bābājī replied, "You will recognize him by his eyes. You must accept him because he will be the continuation of the lineage." From his first meeting with young Prabhuji, Guru Mahārāja recognized him and officially initiated him as his disciple. For Prabhuji, this initiation marked the beginning of the most intense and mature stage of his retroprogressive process. Under the guidance of Guru Mahārāja, he studied Advaita Vedanta and deepened his meditation. Since his guru was a great devotee of Śrī Rāmakṛṣṇa Paramahaṁsa and Śāradā Devī, Prabhuji desired to be initiated into this disciplic lineage. He sought initiation from Swami Swahananda (1921–2012), minister and spiritual leader of the Vedanta Society of Southern California from 1976 to 2012. Swami Swahananda was a disciple of Swami Vijñānānanda, a direct disciple of Rāmakṛṣṇa. In 2008, Swami Swahananda initiated him, granting him both *dīkṣā* and the blessings of Śrī Rāmakṛṣṇa and the Divine Mother.

Guru Mahārāja guided Prabhuji until he officially bestowed upon him the sacraments of the sacred order of *avadhūtas*. In March 2011, H.D.G. Avadhūta Śrī Brahmānanda Bābājī Mahārāja ordered Prabhuji, on behalf of his own master, to accept the responsibility of continuing the lineage of *avadhūtas*. With this title, Prabhuji is the official representative of the line of this disciplic succession for the present generation.

Besides his *dikṣā-gurus*, Prabhuji studied with important spiritual and religious personalities, such as H.H. Swami Yajñavālkyānanda, H.H. Swami Dayānanda Sarasvatī, H.H. Swami Viṣṇu Devānanda Sarasvatī, H.H. Swami Jyotirmayānanda Sarasvatī, H.H. Swami Kṛṣṇānanda Sarasvatī from the Divine Life Society, H.H. Ma Yoga Śakti, H.H. Swami Pratyagbodhānanda, H.H. Swami Mahādevānanda, H.H. Swami Swahānanda of the Ramakrishna Mission, H.H. Swami Adhyātmānanda, H.H. Swami Svarūpanānda, and H.H. Swami Viditātmānanda of the Arsha Vidya Gurukulam, while the wisdom of tantra was awakened in Prabhuji by H.G. Mātājī Rīnā Śarmā in India.

In Vrindavan, he studied the bhakti yoga path in depth with H.H. Narahari Dāsa Bābājī Mahārāja, disciple of H.H. Nityānanda Dāsa Bābājī Mahārāja of Vraja. He also studied bhakti yoga with various disciples of H.D.G. A.C. Bhaktivedānta Swami Prabhupāda: H.H. Kapīndra Swami, H.H. Paramadvaiti Mahārāja, H.H. Jagajīvana Dāsa, H.H. Tamāla Kṛṣṇa Gosvāmī, H.H. Bhagavān Dāsa Mahārāja, and H.H. Kīrtanānanda Swami, among others.

In 1980, Prabhuji received the blessings of H.G. Mother Krishnabai, the famous disciple of H.D.G. Swami Rāmdās. In 1984, he learned and began to practice Maharishi Mahesh Yogi's Transcendental Meditation technique. In 1988, he took the *kriyā-yoga* course on Paramahaṁsa Yogānanda. After two years, he was officially initiated into the technique of *kriyā-yoga* by the Self-Realization Fellowship. In 1982 he received *dikṣā* from H.H. Kīrtanānanda Swami, disciple of Śrīla Prabhupāda, who also gave him his second initiation in 1991 and *sannyāsa* initiation in 1993.

Prabhuji wanted to confirm the sacraments of the holy order of *sannyāsa* also within the Advaita Vedanta lineage. His *sannyāsa-dīkṣā* was confirmed on August 11, 1995, by H.H. Swami Jyotirmayānanda Sarasvatī, founder of the Yoga Research Foundation and disciple of H.H. Swami Śivānanda Sarasvatī of Rishikesh.

Prabhuji has been honored with various titles and diplomas by many leaders of prestigious religious and spiritual institutions in India. He was given the honorable title Kṛṣṇa Bhakta by H.H. Swami Viṣṇu Devānanda (the only title of Bhakti Yoga given by Swami Viṣṇu), disciple of H.H. Swami Śivānanda Sarasvatī and the founder of the Sivananda Organization. He was given the title Bhaktivedānta by H.H. B.A. Paramadvaiti Mahārāja, the founder of Vrinda. He was given the title Yogācārya by H.H. Swami Viṣṇu Devānanda, the Paramanand Institute of Yoga Sciences and Research of Indore, India, the International Yoga Federation, the Indian Association of Yoga, and the Śrī Shankarananda Yogashram of Mysore, India. He received the respectable title Śrī Śrī Rādhā Śyam Sunder Pāda-Padma Bhakta Śiromaṇi directly from H.H. Satyanārāyaṇa Dāsa Bābājī Mahant of the Chatu Vaiṣṇava Sampradāya.

Prabhuji dedicated more than forty years to studying hatha yoga with prestigious masters of classical and traditional yoga, such as H.H. Bapuji, H.H. Swami Viṣṇu Devānanda Sarasvatī, H.H. Swami Jyotirmayānanda Sarasvatī, H.H. Swami Satchidānanda Sarasvatī, H.H. Swami Vignānānanda Sarasvatī, and Śrī Madana-mohana.

He attended several systematic hatha yoga teacher training courses at prestigious institutions until he achieved the level of Master Ācārya. He has completed studies at the following institutions: World Yoga University, the Sivananda Yoga Vedanta, the Ananda Ashram, the Yoga Research Foundation, the Integral Yoga Academy, the Patanjala Yoga Kendra, the Ma Yoga Shakti International Mission, the Prana Yoga Organization, the Rishikesh Yoga Peeth, the Swami Sivananda Yoga Research Center, and the Swami Sivananda Yogasana Research Center.

Prabhuji is a member of the Indian Association of Yoga, Yoga Alliance ERYT 500 and YACEP, the International Association of Yoga Therapists, and the International Yoga Federation. In 2014, the International Yoga Federation honored him with the position of Honorary Member of the World Yoga Council.

His interest in the complex anatomy of the human body led him to study chiropractic at the prestigious Institute of Health of the Back and Extremities in Tel Aviv, Israel. In 1993, he received a diploma from Dr. Sheinerman, the founder and director of the institute.

Later, he earned a massage therapy diploma at the Academy of Western Galilee. The knowledge he acquired in this field deepened his understanding of hatha yoga and contributed to the creation of his own method.

Retroprogressive Yoga is the result of Prabhuji's efforts to improve his practice and teaching methods. It is a system based especially on the teachings of his gurus and the sacred scriptures. Prabhuji has systematized various traditional yoga techniques to create a methodology suitable for Western audiences. Retroprogressive Yoga aspires to the experience of our authentic nature, promoting balance, health, and flexibility through proper diet, cleansing techniques, preparations (*āyojanas*), sequences (*vinyāsas*), postures (*āsanas*), breathing exercises (*prāṇayama*), relaxation (*śavāsana*), meditation (*dhyāna*), and exercises with locks (*bandhas*) and seals (*mudras*) to direct and empower *prāṇa*.

Since his childhood and throughout his life, Prabhuji has been an enthusiastic admirer, student, and practitioner of classic karate-do. From the age of 13, he studied different styles in Chile, such as kenpo with Sensei Arturo Petit and kung-fu, but specialized in the most traditional Japanese style of shotokan. He received the rank of black belt (third dan) from Shihan Kenneth Funakoshi (ninth dan). He also learned from Sensei Takahashi (seventh dan) and Sensei Masataka Mori (ninth dan). Additionally, he practiced shorin ryu style with Sensei Enrique Daniel Welcher (seventh dan), who granted him the rank of black belt (second dan).

Through karate-do, he delved into Buddhism and gained additional knowledge about the physics of motion. He is a member of Funakoshi's Shotokan Karate Association.

Prabhuji grew up in an artistic environment and his love of painting began to develop in his childhood. His father, the renowned Chilean painter Yosef Har-Zion ZT"L, motivated him to devote himself to art. He learned painting from both his father and the famous Chilean painter Marcelo Cuevas. Prabhuji's abstract paintings reflect the depths of the spirit.

Since he was a young boy, Prabhuji has been especially drawn to postal stamps, postcards, mailboxes, postal transportation systems, and all mail-related activities. He has taken every opportunity to visit post offices in different cities and countries. He has delved into the study of philately, the field of collecting, sorting, and studying postage stamps. This passion led him to become a professional philatelist, a stamp distributor authorized by the American Philatelic Society, and a member of the following societies: the Royal Philatelic Society London, the Royal Philatelic Society of Victoria, the United States Stamp Society, the Great Britain Philatelic Society, the American Philatelic Society, the Society of Israel Philatelists, the Society for Hungarian Philately, the National Philatelic Society UK, the Fort Orange Stamp Club, the American Stamp Dealers Association, the US Philatelic Classics Society, Filabras - Associação dos Filatelistas Brasileiros, and the Collectors Club of NYC.

Based on his extensive knowledge of philately, theology, and Eastern philosophy, Prabhuji created "Meditative Philately" or "Philatelic Yoga," a spiritual practice that uses philately as the basis for practicing attention, concentration, observation, and meditation. It is inspired by the ancient Hindu mandala meditation and it can lead the practitioner to elevated states of consciousness, deep relaxation, and concentration that fosters the recognition of consciousness. Prabhuji wrote his thesis on this new type of yoga, "Meditative Philately," attracting the interest of the Indian academic community due to its innovative way of connecting meditation with different hobbies and activities. For this thesis, he was honored with a PhD in Yogic Philosophy from Yoga-Samskrutham University.

For more than 20 years, Prabhuji lived in Israel, where he furthered his studies of Judaism. One of his main teachers and sources of inspiration was Rabbi Shalom Dov Lifshitz ZT"L, whom he met in 1997. This great saint guided him for several years along the intricate paths of the Torah and Hassidism. He personally taught him Tanakh, Talmud, Midrash, Shulchan Aruch, Mishneh Torah, Tanya, Kabbalah and Zohar. The two developed a very close relationship. Prabhuji also studied the Talmud with Rabbi Raphael Rapaport Shlit"a (Ponovich), Hassidism with Rabbi Israel Lifshitz Shlit"a, and the Torah with Rabbi Daniel Sandler Shlit"a. Prabhuji is a great devotee of Rabbi Mordechai Eliyahu ZT"L, who personally blessed him.

Prabhuji visited the United States in 2000 and during his stay in New York, he realized that it was the most appropriate place to found a religious organization. He was particularly attracted by the pluralism and respectful attitude of American society toward freedom of religion. He was impressed by the deep respect of both the public and the government for religious minorities. After consulting his masters and requesting their blessings, Prabhuji relocated to the United States. In 2003, the Prabhuji Mission was born, a Hindu church aimed at preserving Prabhuji's universal and pluralistic vision of Hinduism and his "Retroprogressive Path."

Although he did not seek to attract followers, for 15 years (1995–2010), Prabhuji considered the requests of a few people who approached him asking to become his monastic disciples. Those who chose to see him as their spiritual master voluntarily accepted vows of poverty and life-long dedication to spiritual practice (*sadhāna*), religious devotion (*bhakti*), and selfless service (*seva*). Although he no longer accepts new disciples, he continues to guide the small group of monastic disciples of the contemplative Ramakrishnananda Monastic Order that he founded.

In 2011, Prabhuji founded the Avadhutashram (monastery) in the Catskills Mountains in upstate New York, USA. The Avadhutashram is his hermitage, the residence of the monastic disciples of the Ramakrishnananda Order, and the headquarters of the Prabhuji Mission. He operates various humanitarian projects, inspired in his experience that "serving the part is serving the Whole." The ashram organizes humanitarian projects such as the Prabhuji Food Distribution Program and the Prabhuji Toy Distribution Program.

According to Prabhuji, the quest for the Self is individual, solitary, personal, private, and intimate. It is not a collective endeavor to be undertaken through organized, institutional, or communitarian religiosity. Nowadays, he disagrees with spirituality practiced in a social, communal, or collective manner. Therefore, he does not proselytize or preach, nor does he try to persuade, convince, or make anyone change their perspective, philosophy, or religion. His message does not promote collective spirituality, but individual inner search.

Prabhuji has delegated the choice to his disciples between keeping his teachings exclusively within the monastic order or spreading his message to the public. Upon the explicit request of his disciples, he has agreed to have his books published and his lectures disseminated, as long as this does not compromise his privacy and his life as a hermit.

In 2022, Prabhuji founded the Retroprogressive Institute. Here, his most senior disciples can systematically share his teachings and message through video conferences. The institute offers support and help for a deeper understanding of his teachings.

In 2025, he established the Retroprogressive Yoga Academy, where he personally transmits his yoga method to disciples and students without departing from his hermitic life. That same year, he founded the Retroprogressive Karate Academy, through which he shares his knowledge of the martial arts as a path toward the expansion of consciousness.

Prabhuji is a respected member of the American Philosophical Association, the American Association of Philosophy Teachers, the American Association of University Professors, the Southwestern Philosophical Society, the Authors Guild, the National Writers Union, PEN America, the International Writers Association, the National Association of Independent Writers and Editors, the National Writers Association, the Alliance Independent Authors, and the Independent Book Publishers Association.

Prabhuji's vast literary contribution includes books in Spanish, English, and Hebrew, such as *Kundalini Yoga: The Power is in you*, *What is, as it is*, *Bhakti Yoga: The Path of Love*, *Tantra: Liberation in the World*, *Experimenting with the Truth*, *Advaita Vedanta: Being the Self*, *Yoga: Union with reality*, commentaries on the *Īśāvāsya Upanishad and the Diamond Sūtra*, *I am that I am*, *The Symbolic Turn*, *Being*, *Questioning your Answers: Philosophy as a Question*, *Beyond Answers: Philosophy in the Eternal Search*, *Phenomenology of the Sacred: Foundations for a Retroprogressive Phenomenology*, *Discovering the Last God*, and *Mapuche Spirituality*.

The term *PRABHUJI*
by Swami Ramananda

Several years ago, some disciples, followers and friends of His Holiness Avadhūta Bhaktivedānta Yogācārya Śrī Ramakrishnananda Bābājī Mahārāja, opted to refer to him as Prabhuji. In this article, I would like to clarify the deep meaning of this Sanskrit term. The word *prabhu* in Sanskrit means "a master, lord or a king" and it is applied in the scriptures to God and to the Guru.

Like many words in the Sanskrit language, the word is actually made of some components, and understanding its etymology will lead us to discover its various meanings. The word *prabhu* is a combination of the root *bhu* which means "to become, to exist, to be, to live" and the prefix *pra*, which can mean "forth, or forward" and which then, when attached to *bhu* would mean "one who causes to exist, who gives life, from whom life emanates, that which sustains or maintains."

The prefix *pra* can also mean "very much, or supremacy," and then when attached to the root *bhu* would mean "to be the master, to rule over."

The suffix *jī* is an honorific title in Hindi and other Indian languages. It is added after the names of Gods and esteemed personalities to show respect and reverence.

As manifestations of the Divine, great *ṛṣis*, or 'seers' and gurus are also called *prabhus*. For example, the sage Nārada is addressing the *ṛṣi* Vyasadeva as prabhu:

जिज्ञासितमधीतं च ब्रह्म यत्तत्सनातनम् ।
तथापि शोचस्यात्मानमकृतार्थ इव प्रभो ॥

> *jijñāsitam adhītaṁ ca*
> *brahma yat tat sanātanam*
> *tathāpi śocasy ātmānam*
> *akṛtārtha iva prabho*

You have fully delineated the subject of impersonal Brahman as well as the knowledge derived therefrom. Why should you be despondent in spite of all this, thinking that you are undone, my dear master (*prabhu*)?

(*Bhāgavata Purāṇa*, 1.5.4)

Mahārāja Parīkṣit addresses Śukadeva as *prabhu* when he approaches the sage to seek spiritual guidance, thus accepting him as his guru.

यच्छ्रोतव्यमथो जप्यं यत्कर्तव्यं नृभिः प्रभो ।
स्मर्तव्यं भजनीयं वा ब्रूहि यद्वा विपर्ययम् ॥

yac chrotavyam atho japyaṁ
yat kartavyaṁ nṛbhiḥ prabho
smartavyaṁ bhajanīyaṁ vā
brūhi yad vā viparyayam

O prabhu, please let me know what a man should hear, chant, remember and worship, and also what he should not do. Please explain all this to me.

(*Bhāgavata Purana*, 1.19.38)

The term *avadhūta*

This is an excerpt from the book *Sannyāsa Darśana* by Swami Niranjanānanda Sarasvatī, a disciple of Paramahaṁsa Swami Satyānanda.

Stages of *sannyāsāvadhūta*

"The *avadhūta* represents the pinnacle of spiritual evolution; none is superior to him. *Avadhūta* means 'one who is immortal' (*akṣara*) and who has totally discarded worldly ties. He is really Brahman itself. He has realized he is pure intelligence and is not concerned about the six frailties of human birth, namely: sorrow, delusion, old age, death, hunger, and thirst. He has shaken off all bondage of the experimental world and roams freely like a child, a madman or one possessed by spirits.

He may be with or without clothes. He wears no distinctive emblem of any order. He has no desire to sleep, beg, or bathe. He views his body as a corpse and subsists on the food that comes to him from all classes. He does not interpret the *śāstras* or the Vedas. For him, nothing is righteous or unrighteous, holy or unholy.

He is free from karma. The karmas of this life and past lives are all burned out, and due to the absence of *kartṛtva* (the doer) and *bhoktṛtva* (the desire for enjoyment), no future karmas are created. Only the *prārabdha-karmas* (unalterable) that have already begun to operate will affect his body, helping to sustain it, but his mind will remain unaffected. He will live in this world until the *prārabdha-karmas* are extinguished, and then his body will fall. Then he is said to attain *videhamukti* (the state beyond body consciousness).

Such a liberated soul never returns to the embodied state. He is not born again; he is immortal. He has achieved the final aim of being born in this world."

The *Bṛhad-avadhūta Upanishad* reads as follows: "The *avadhūta* is so called because he is immortal; he is the greatest; he has discarded worldly ties, and he is alluded to in the meaning of the sentence 'Thou art That'."

His Divine Grace Śrīla Bhakti Ballabh Tīrtha Mahārāja in his article entitled "*Pariṣads*: Śrīla Vaṁśi das Bābājī" wrote: "He was a Paramahaṁsa Vaiṣṇava who acted in the manner of an *avadhūta*. The word *avadhūta* refers to one who has shaken off from himself all worldly feelings and obligations. He does not care for social conventions, especially the *varṇāśrama-dharma*, that is, he is quite eccentric in his behavior. Nityānanda Prabhu is often characterized as an *avadhūta*."

From the foreword to Dattātreya's *Avadhūta-gītā*, translated and annotated by Swami Aśokānanda: "The *Avadhūta-gītā* is a Vedanta text representing extreme Advaita or non-dualism. It is attributed to Dattātreya, who is looked upon as an Incarnation of God.

Unfortunately, we possess no historical data concerning when or where he was born, how long he lived, or how he arrived at the knowledge disclosed in the text.

Avadhūta means a liberated soul, one who has 'passed away from' or 'shaken off' all worldly attachments and cares and has attained a spiritual state equivalent to the existence of God. Although *avadhūta* naturally implies renunciation, it includes an additional and even higher state that is neither attachment nor detachment, but is beyond both. An *avadhūta* feels no need to observe any rules, whether secular or religious. He seeks nothing and avoids nothing. He has neither knowledge nor ignorance. Having realized that he is the infinite Self, he lives in that vivid realization."

Swami Vivekānanda, one of the greatest advaitins of all times, often quoted this *Gītā*. He once said, "Men like the one who wrote this song keep religion alive. They have experienced. They care for nothing, and feel nothing done to the body; they don't care for heat, cold, danger, or anything else. They sit still, enjoying the bliss of the Ātman, and even if embers burn their bodies, they do not feel them."

The *Avadhūta Upanishad* is number 79 in the *Muktikā* canon of Upanishads. It is a *Sannyāsa Upanishad* associated with the Black (Kṛṣṇa) Yajur-veda: "One who has transcended the *varṇāśrama* system and has always established in himself, that yogi, who is above the *varṇāśrama* divisions, is called *avadhūta*." (*Avadhūta Upanishad*, 2).

The *Brahma-nirvāṇa Tantra* book describes how to identify *avadhūtas* of the following types:

- *Bramhāvadhūta*: An *avadhūta* by birth, who appears in any cast of society and is completely indifferent to the world or worldly matters.
- *Śaivāvadhūta*: *Avadhūtas* who have taken to the renounced order of life or *sannyāsa*, often with long matted hair (*jaṭa*), or who dress in the manner of Shaivites and spend almost all of their time in trance *samādhi*, or meditation.
- *Virāvadhūta*: This person looks like a *sadhū* who has put red-colored sandal paste on his body and wears saffron-colored clothes. His hair is very well grown and is normally furling in the wind. They wear around their necks a *rudrākṣa-mālā* or a chain of bones. They carry a wooden stick, or *daṇḍa*, in their hand, and additionally always carry an axe (*paraśu*) or an *ḍamaru* (small drum) with them.
- *Kulāvadhūta*: These people are supposed to have taken the Kaul *Sampradāya* initiation. It is very difficult to recognize these people as they do not wear any outward signs that can identify them from others. The specialty of these people is that they stay and live like normal people. They may show themselves in the form of kings or family men.

The *Nātha Sampradāya* is a form of *Avadhūta-pantha* (sect). In this *Sampradāya*, Guru and yoga are of extreme importance. Therefore, the most important book of this *Sampradāya* is the *Avadhūta-gītā*. Śrī Gorakṣanāth is considered the highest form of the *avadhūta* state.

The nature of *avadhūta* is the subject of the *Avadhūta-gītā*, traditionally attributed to Dattātreya.

According to Bipin Joshi, the main characteristics of an *avadhūta* are: "He who is a sinless philosopher and has cast off the shackles of ignorance (*ajñāna*). He who lives in a stateless state and relishes the experience all the time. He revels in this blissful state, unperturbed by the material world. In this unique state, the *avadhūta* is neither awake nor in deep sleep; there is no sign of life or death. It is a state defying all descriptions. It is the state of infinite bliss, which a finite language is incapable of describing. It can only be intuited purely by our intellect. A state that is neither truth nor non-truth, neither existence nor nonexistence. He who has realized his identity with the imperishable, who possesses incomparable excellence, who has shaken off the bonds of *saṁsāra* and never deviates from his goal. That thou art (*tat tvam asi*), and other upanishadic statements, are ever present in the mind of such an enlightened soul. That sage who is rooted in the plenary experience of 'Verily, I am Brahman (*ahaṁ Brahmāsmi*)', 'All this is Brahman (*sarvaṁ khalvidaṁ brahma*)', and that '…there is no plurality, I and God are one and the same…', etc. Supported by the personal experience of such Vedic statements, he moves freely in a state of total bliss. Such a person is a renunciant, liberated, *avadhūta*, yogi, paramahamsa, *brāhmaṇa*."

From Wikipedia, the free encyclopedia:

Avadhūta is a Sanskrit term used in Indian religions to refer to mystics or antinomian saints who are beyond ego-consciousness, duality, and common worldly concerns, and act without consideration of standard social etiquette. Such personalities "roam free as a child on the face of the Earth." An *avadhūta* does not identify with his mind or body or 'names and forms' (Sanskrit: *nāma-rūpa*). Such a person is considered pure consciousness (Sanskrit: *caitanya*) in human form.

Avadhūtas play a significant role in the history, origins, and rejuvenation of a number of traditions such as yoga, Advaita Vedanta, Buddhist, and bhakti *paramparās* even as they are released from standard observances. *Avadhūtas* are the voice of the *avadhūti*, the channel that resolves the dichotomy of *Vāmācāra* and *Dakṣiṇācāra* or "left and right-handed traditions." An *avadhūta* may or may not continue to practice religious rites as long as they are free from sectarian ritual observance and affiliation. The Monier Williams Sanskrit dictionary defines the term *avadhūta* as follows: "अवधूत / अव-धूत — one who has shaken off from himself worldly feelings and obligations."

From *Hinduism, an alphabetical guide* by Roshen Dalal

Avadhūta: A term for a liberated soul, one who has renounced the world. Totally beyond all that is, an *avadhūta* follows no rules, no fixed practices, and has no need to follow conventional norms. There are several texts dealing with the life and nature of an *avadhūta*. In the *Avadhūta Upanishad*, the Ṛṣi Dattātreya describes the nature of the *avadhūta*. Such a person is immortal, has discarded all worldly ties, and is always full of bliss. One of its verses states: "Let thought contemplate Viṣṇu, or let it be dissolved in the bliss of Brahman. I, the witness, do nothing, nor do I cause anything to be done." (v.28)

The *Turīyātīta Avadhūta Upanishad* contains a description of the *avadhūta* who has reached the state of consciousness beyond the *turīya*. In this state, a person is pure, detached and totally free. An *avadhūta* who has reached this level does not chant mantras or practice rituals, wears no caste marks, and is finished with all religious and secular duties. He wears no clothes and eats whatever comes his way. He wanders alone, observing silence, and is totally absorbed in non-duality. The *Avadhūta-gītā* has similar descriptions.

The *Uddhava-gītā*, which is part of the *Bhāgavata Purāṇa*, describes an *avadhūta* who learned from all aspects of life and was at home anywhere in the world. The term *avadhūta* can be applied to any liberated person, but it also refers specifically to a *sannyāsa* sect.

Avadhūta Upanishad

Avadhūta Upanishad is a small Upanishad consisting of about 32 mantras. It falls under the category of the *Sannyāsa Upanishads* and is a part of Kṛṣṇa Yajurveda. The *Avadhūta Upanishad* takes the form of a dialogue between Dattātreya and Ṛṣi Saṁkṛti.

One day Ṛṣi Saṁkṛti asks Dattātreya the following questions: "Who is an *avadhūta*?; What is his state?; What are the signs of the *avadhūta*?; How does he live?"

The following are the answers given by the compassionate Dattātreya.

Who is an *avadhūta*?

The *avadhūta* is so called because he is beyond any decay; he lives freely according to his will, he destroys the bondage of worldly desires, and his only goal is That thou Art (*tat tvam asi*).

The *avadhūta* goes far beyond all the castes (such as *brāhmaṇa, vaiśya, kṣatrya,* and *śūdra*) and *Āśramas* (such as *brāmhacaryā, gṛhastha, vānaprastha,* and *sannyāsa*). He is the highest Yogi who is established in a constant state of self-realization.

What is his state?

An *avadhūta* always enjoys supreme bliss. The divine joy represents his head, happiness is his right wing, ecstasy represents his left wing, and bliss is his very nature. The life of an *avadhūta* shows extreme detachment.

What are the signs of *avadhūta*? How does he live?

An *avadhūta* lives according to his own will. He may wear clothes or go naked. For him, there is no difference between *dharma* or *adharma*, sacrifice or non-sacrifice, because he is beyond these aspects. He performs inner sacrifice and that forms their *aśvamedha-yajña*. He is a great yogi who remains unaffected even when engaged in worldly objects. He remains pure.

The ocean accepts water from all the rivers but remains unchanged. Similarly, an *avadhūta* is unaffected by worldly objects. He is always at peace and (like the ocean), all his desires are absorbed in this supreme peace.

For an *avadhūta* there is no birth or death, no bondage or liberation. He may have performed various actions for the sake of liberation, but they become history once he becomes an *avadhūta*. He is always satisfied. Others wander to fulfill their desires. But an *avadhūta*, being already satisfied, does not run after any desire. Others perform various rituals for the sake of heaven, but an *avadhūta* is already established in the omnipresent state and hence needs no rituals.

Other qualified teachers spend time teaching the scriptures (Vedas) but *avadhūta* goes beyond those activities, because he has no actions. He doesn't have any desire to sleep, beg (*bhikṣa*), bathe, or clean.

An *avadhūta* is always free from doubt, and since he is always in union with the supreme reality, he does not even need to meditate. Meditation is for those people who are not yet one with God, but an *avadhūta* is always in the state of union and therefore does not need to meditate.

Those who are after *karmas* (actions) are filled with *vāsanās*. These *vāsanās* haunt them even when they finish their *prārabdha-karma*. Ordinary men meditate because they wish to fulfill their desires. However, an *avadhūta* always stays away from that trap. His mind is beyond mental destruction and *samādhi*. Mental destruction as well as *samādhi* are possibly modifications of the mind. The *avadhūta* is already eternal and hence, there is nothing to attain for him.

Following worldly duties is like an arrow released from a bow, i.e. it cannot be stopped from giving good or bad fruits causing a cycle of action-reaction. However, an *avadhūta* is not a doer at any level and is not engaged in any action.

Having attained such a stage of detachment, an *avadhūta* remains unaffected even if he follows a way of life as prescribed by the scriptures. Even if he engages in *actions* such as worshipping God, bathing, begging, etc., he remains unattached to them. He lives as a witness and therefore does not perform any action.

An *avadhūta* can clearly see Brahman before his eyes. He is free from ignorance or *māyā*. He has no actions left to be performed and nothing left to achieve. He is totally satisfied and there is no one else with whom he can be compared.

नलिनी नालिनी नासे गन्ध: सौरभ उच्यते ।
घ्राणोऽवधूतो मुख्यास्यं विपणो वाग्रसविद्रस: ॥

nalinī nālinī nāse
gandhaḥ saurabha ucyate
ghrāṇo 'vadhūto mukhyāsyaṁ
vipaṇo vāg rasavid rasaḥ

The two doors called Nalinī and Nālinī are to be known as the two nostrils, and the city named Saurabha represents the aroma. The companion spoken of as *avadhūta* is the sense of smell. The door called Mukhyā is the mouth, and Vipaṇa is the faculty of speech. Rasajña is the sense of taste.
(*Bhāgavata Purāṇa*, 4.29.11)

Purport of H.D.G. A.C. Bhaktivedanta Swami Prabhupada:

The word *avadhūta* means "most free." A person is not under the rules and regulations of any injunction when he has attained the stage of *avadhūta*. In other words, he can act as he likes. This stage of *avadhūta* is exactly like air, which does not care for any obstruction. In the Bhagavad Gita (6.34) it is said:

चञ्चलं हि मन: कृष्ण प्रमाथि बलवद्दृढम् ।
तस्याहं निग्रहं मन्ये वायोरिव सुदुष्करम् ॥

> *cañcalaṁ hi manaḥ kṛṣṇa*
> *pramāthi balavad dṛḍham*
> *tasyāhaṁ nigrahaṁ manye*
> *vāyor iva suduṣkaram*

The mind is restless, turbulent, obstinate, and very strong, O Kṛṣṇa, and to subdue it is, it seems to me, more difficult than controlling the wind.
(Bhagavad Gita, 6.34)

Just as air or wind cannot be stopped by anyone, the two nostrils, situated in one place, enjoy the sense of smell without impediment. With the tongue, the mouth continuously tastes all kinds of tasty foods.

अक्षरत्वाद्वरेण्यत्वाद्धूतसंसारबन्धनात् ।
तत्त्वमस्यर्थसिद्धत्वात् अवधूतोऽभिधीयते ॥

> *akṣaratvād vareṇyatvād*
> *dhūta-saṁsāra-bandhanāt*
> *tat tvam asy-artha siddhatvāt*
> *avadhūto 'bhidhīyate*

Since he is immutable (*akṣara*), the most excellent (*vareṇya*), since he has removed the worldly attachments (*dhūta-samsāra-bandanāt*) and he has realized the meaning of *tat tvam asi* (That thou art), he is called *avadhūta*.

(*Kulārṇava Tantra*, 17.24)

From Yogapedia: What does *avadhūta* mean?

Avadhūta is a Sanskrit term used to refer to a person who has reached a stage in their spiritual development in which they are beyond worldly concerns. People who have reached the stage of *avadhūta* may act without considering common social etiquette or their own ego. This term is often used in the cases of mystics or saints.

Advanced yoga practitioners may find inspiration in the idea of reaching this stage through further sustained meditation and asana practice.

Avadhūta is often associated with some sort of eccentric and spontaneous behavior from a holy person. This comes partly from the fact that mystics who have achieved this level of spiritual enlightenment may forget wearing clothes or other normal social behavior.

About the Prabhuji Mission

Prabhuji Mission is a Hindu religious, spiritual, and charitable organization founded by H.H. Avadhūta Bhaktivedānta Yogācārya Śrī Ramakrishnananda Bābājī Mahārāja. Its purpose is to preserve the "Retroprogressive Path," which reflects Prabhuji's vision of *Sanātana-dharma* and advocates for the global awakening of consciousness as the radical solution to humanity's problems.

Apart from imparting religious and spiritual teachings, the organization carries out extensive philanthropic work in the USA, based on the principles of karma yoga, selfless work performed with dedication to God.

Prabhuji Mission was established in 2003 in the USA as a Hindu church aimed at preserving its founder's universal and pluralistic vision of Hinduism.

The Prabhuji Mission operates a Hindu temple called Śrī Śrī Bhagavān Yeshua Jagat Jananī Miriam Premānanda Mandir, which offers worship and religious ceremonies to parishioners. The extensive library of the Retroprogressive Institute provides its teachers with abundant study materials to research the various theologies and philosophies explored by Prabhuji in his books and lectures.

The Avadhutashram monastery educates monastic disciples on various aspects of Prabhuji's approach to Hinduism and offers them the opportunity to express devotion to God through devotional service by selflessly contributing their skills and training to the Mission's programs.

The Mission publishes and distributes Prabhuji's books and lectures and operates humanitarian projects such as the "Prabhuji Food Distribution Program," a weekly event in which dozens of families in need from Upstate New York receive fresh and nutritious food and the "Prabhuji Toy Distribution Program," which provides the less privileged kids with abundance of Christmas gifts.

Avadhutashram
Round Top, Nueva York, EE. UU.

About the Avadhutashram

The Avadhutashram (monastery) was founded by Prabhuji. It is the headquarters of the Prabhuji Mission and the hermitage of H.H. Avadhūta Bhaktivedānta Yogācārya Śrī Ramakrishnananda Bābājī Mahārāja and his monastic disciples of the Ramakrishnananda Contemplative Monastic Order.

The ideals of the Avadhutashram are love and selfless service, based on the universal vision that God is in everything and everyone. Its mission is to distribute spiritual books and organize humanitarian projects such as the Prabhuji Food Distribution Program and the Prabhuji Toy Distribution Program.

The Avadhutashram is not commercial and operates without soliciting donations. Its activities are funded by Prabhuji's Gifts, a non-profit company founded by Prabhuji, which sells esoteric items from different traditions that he himself has used for spiritual practices during his evolutionary process. Its mission is to preserve and disseminate traditional religious, mystical, and ancestral crafts.

The Retroprogressive Path

The Retroprogressive Path does not require you to be part of a group or a member of an organization, institution, society, congregation, club, or exclusive community. Living in a temple, monastery, or *āśram* is not mandatory, because it is not about a change of residence, but of consciousness. It does not urge you to believe, but to doubt. It does not demand you to accept something, but to explore, investigate, examine, inquire, and question everything. It does not suggest being what you should be but being what you really are.

The Retroprogressive Path supports freedom of expression but not proselytizing. This route does not promise answers to our questions but induces us to question our answers. It does not promise to be what we are not or to attain what we have not already achieved. It is a retro-evolutionary path of self-discovery that leads us from what we think we are to what we really are. It is not the only way, nor the best, the simplest, or the most direct. It is an involuntary process par excellence that shows what is obvious and undeniable but usually goes unnoticed: that which is simple, innocent, and natural. It is a path that begins and ends in you.

The Retroprogressive Path is a continuous revelation that expands eternally. It delves into consciousness from an ontological perspective, transcending all religion and spiritual paths. It is the discovery of diversity as a unique and inclusive reality. It is the encounter of consciousness with itself, aware of itself and its own reality. In fact, this path is a simple invitation to dance in the now, to love the present moment, and to celebrate our authenticity. It is an unconditional proposal to stop living as a victim of circumstance and to live as a passionate adventurer. It is a call to return to the place we have never left, without offering us anything we do not already possess or teaching us anything we do not already know. It is a call for an inner revolution and to enter the fire of life that only consumes dreams, illusions, and fantasies but does not touch what we are. It does not help us reach our desired goal, but instead prepares us for the unexpected miracle.

This path was nurtured over a lifetime dedicated to the search for Truth. It is a grateful offering to existence for what I have received. But remember, do not look for me. Look for yourself. It is not me you need, because you are the only one who really matters. This life is just a wonderful parenthesis in eternity to know and love. What you yearn for lies in you, here and now, as what you really are.

Your unconditional well-wisher,
Prabhuji

Prabhuji today

Prabhuji has retired from public life

Prabhuji is the sole disciple of H.D.G. Avadhūta Śrī Brahmānanda Bābājī Mahārāja, who is himself one of the closest and most intimate disciples of H.D.G. Avadhūta Śrī Mastarāma Bābājī Mahārāja.

Guru Mahārāja guided Prabhuji until he officially bestowed upon him the sacraments of the sacred order of *avadhūtas*. Prabhuji was appointed as the successor of the lineage by his master, who conferred upon him the responsibility of continuing the line of disciplic succession of *avadhūtas*, or the sacred *paramparā*, officially designating him as guru and commanding him to serve as the successor Ācārya under the name H.H. Avadhūta Bhaktivedānta Yogācārya Śrī Ramakrishnananda Bābājī Mahārāja.

Prabhuji is also a disciple of H.D.G. Bhakti-kavi Atulānanda Ācārya Mahārāja, who is a direct disciple of H.D.G. A.C. Bhaktivedānta Swami Prabhupāda.

In 2011, with the blessings of his Gurudeva, he adopted the path of a secluded *bhajanānandī* and withdrew from society to lead the contemplative life of a hermit. Since then, he has been living as an independent Messianic-Marian Hindu religious hermit. His days have been spent in solitude, praying, writing, painting, and meditating in silence and contemplation.

He no longer participates in *sat-saṅgs*, lectures, gatherings, meetings, retreats, seminars, study groups, or courses. We ask everyone to respect his privacy and do not try to contact him by any means for gatherings, meetings, interviews, blessings, *śaktipāta*, initiations, or personal visits.

Prabhuji's teachings

As an *avadhūta* and a realized master, Prabhuji has always appreciated the essence and wisdom of a wide variety of religious practices from around the world. Although many see him as an enlightened being, Prabhuji has no intention of presenting himself as a public figure, preacher, propagator of beliefs, promoter of philosophies, guide, coach, content creator, influencer, preceptor, mentor, counselor, consultant, monitor, tutor, teacher, instructor, educator, enlightener, pedagogue, evangelist, rabbi, *posek halacha*, healer, therapist, satsangist, pointer, psychic, leader, medium, savior, New Age guru, or authority of any kind, whether spiritual or material. According to Prabhuji, the quest for the Self is individual, solitary, personal, private, and intimate. It is not a collective endeavor to be undertaken through organized, institutional, or community religiosity. Since 2011, Prabhuji has disagreed with spirituality practiced in a social, communal, or collective manner. Therefore, he does not proselytize or preach, nor does he try to persuade, convince, or make anyone change their perspective, philosophy, or religion. Many may find his insights valuable and apply them partially or fully to their own development, but Prabhuji's teachings should not be interpreted as personal advice, direction, counseling, instruction, guidance, tutoring, self-help methods, or techniques for spiritual, physical, emotional, or psychological development. The proposed teachings do not aspire to be definitive solutions for life's spiritual, material, financial, psychological, emotional, romantic, family, social, or physical problems. Prabhuji does not promise miracles, mystical experiences, astral journeys, healings of any kind, connections with spirits, angels or extraterrestrials, astral travel to other planets, supernatural powers, or spiritual salvation.

Service and glorification of the guru are fundamental spiritual principles in Hinduism. The Prabhuji Mission, as a traditional Hindu church, practices the millenary *guru-bhakti* tradition of reverence to the master.

Some disciples and friends of the Prabhuji Mission, on their own initiative, help to preserve Prabhuji's legacy and his interfaith teachings for future generations by disseminating his books, videos of his internal talks, and websites.

The sacred way

Some time ago, on the sacred journey toward transcendence, Prabhuji reaffirmed his resolve not to disturb those who showed no interest in joining him on this path. This decision is not simple detachment, but instead, a deliberate choice to preserve the essence of this migratory route: a commitment to authenticity and deepening self-inquiry. Such a decision, far from being an abandonment, is a respectful recognition of individual autonomy and divergent destinies and aspirations. On this journey, choosing fellow travelers is not a mere whim, but an exercise in critical discernment and alignment with those whose vision intertwines with own own in the search for our home within our own house.

Public services

Even though the monastery does not accept new residents, volunteers, donations, collaborations, or sponsorships, the public is invited to participate in daily religious services and devotional festivals at the Śrī Śrī Bhagavān Yeshua Jagat Jananī Miriam Premānanda Mandir.

Titles by Prabhuji

What is, as it is: Satsangs with Prabhuji (English)
ISBN-13: 978-1-945894-26-8

Lo que es, tal como es: *Sat-saṅgas* con Prabhuji (Spanish)
ISBN-13: 978-1-945894-27-5
Russian: ISBN-13: 978-1-945894-18-3
Hebrew: ISBN-13: 978-1-945894-24-4

Kundalini Yoga: The Power is in you (English)
ISBN-13: 978-1-945894-30-5

***Kuṇḍalinī-yoga*: El poder está en ti (Spanish)**
ISBN-13: 978-1-945894-31-2

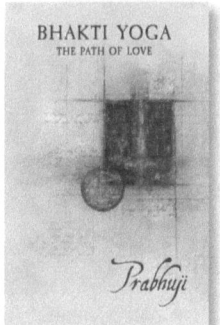

Bhakti Yoga: The Path of Love (English)
ISBN-13: 978-1-945894-28-2

***Bhakti-yoga*: El sendero del amor (Spanish)**
ISBN-13: 978-1-945894-29-9

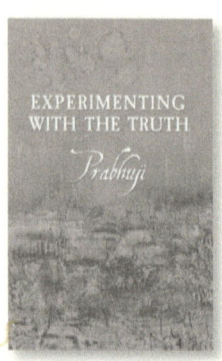

Experimenting with the Truth (English)
ISBN-13: 978-1-945894-32-9

Experimentando con la Verdad (Spanish)
ISBN-13: 978-1-945894-33-6

Hebrew
ISBN-13: 978-1-945894-93-0

Tantra: Liberation in the World (English)
ISBN-13: 978-1-945894-36-7

Tantra: La liberación en el mundo (Spanish)
ISBN-13: 978-1-945894-37-4

Advaita Vedanta: Being the Self (English)
ISBN-13: 978-1-945894-34-3

Advaita Vedānta: **Ser el Ser (Spanish)**
ISBN-13: 978-1-945894-35-0

Beyond Answers: Philosophy in the Eternal Search (English)
ISBN-13: 978-1-945894-91-6

Más allá de las respuestas: La filosofía en la búsqueda eterna (Spanish)
ISBN-13: 978-1-945894-88-6

Discovering the Last God (English)
ISBN-13: 978-1-945894-71-8

Descubriendo el Último Dios (Spanish)
ISBN-13: 978-1-945894-89-3

Questioning your Answers: Philosophy as a Question (English)
ISBN-13: 978-1-945894-80-0

Cuestionando tus respuestas: La filosofía como pregunta (Spanish)
ISBN-13: 978-1-945894-77-0

Īśāvāsya Upanishad
commented by Prabhuji
(**English**)
ISBN-13: 978-1-945894-38-1

Īśāvāsya Upaniṣad
comentado por Prabhuji
(**Spanish**)
ISBN-13: 978-1-945894-40-4

**The Diamond Sūtra
commented by Prabhuji
(English)**
ISBN-13: 978-1-945894-51-0

**El Sūtra del Diamante
comentado por Prabhuji
(Spanish)**
ISBN-13: 978-1-945894-54-1

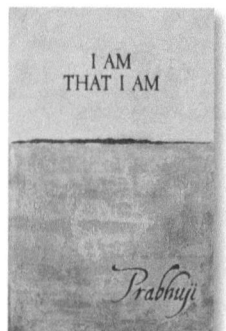

**I am that I am
(English)**
ISBN-13: 978-1-945894-78-7

**Soy el que soy
(Spanish)**
ISBN-13: 978-1-945894-48-0

Being (English)
Vol I: 978-1-945894-73-2
Vol II: 978-1-945894-74-9
Vol III: 978-1-945894-55-8

Ser (Spanish)
Vol I: 978-1-945894-70-1
Vol II: 978-1-945894-94-7
Vol III: 978-1-945894-56-5

The Symbolic Turn (English)
ISBN-13: 978-1-945894-62-6

El giro simbólico (Spanish)
ISBN-13: 978-1-945894-59-6

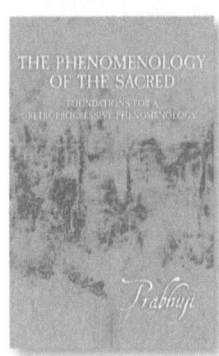

Phenomenology of the Sacred: Foundations for a Retroprogressive Phenomenology (English)
ISBN-13: 978-1-945894-68-8

La fenomenología de lo sagrado: Fundamentos para una Fenomenología Retroprogresiva (Spanish)
ISBN-13: 978-1-945894-65-7

**Mapuche Spirituality
(English)**
ISBN-13: 978-1-945894-92-3

**La espiritualidad mapuche
(Spanish)**
ISBN-13: 978-1-945894-95-4

www.ingramcontent.com/pod-product-compliance
Lightning Source LLC
Chambersburg PA
CBHW020112240426
43673CB00001B/5